Wisdom With
Understanding
is Better
Than Rubies

Marshall M. Fredericks, Sculptor

Marshall M. Fredericks, Sculptor

EDITED BY
Suzanne P. Fredericks

INTRODUCTORY ESSAY BY
Edgar P. Richardson

FOREWORD BY
Samuel Sachs II

RESEARCHED AND COMPILED BY
Marcy Heller Fisher

WITH CONTRIBUTIONS BY
*Barbara Heller, Michaele Duffy Kramer,
Robin R. Salmon, MaryAnn Wilkinson*

MARSHALL M. FREDERICKS SCULPTURE MUSEUM
SAGINAW VALLEY STATE UNIVERSITY
UNIVERSITY CENTER, MICHIGAN | 2003

This book was made possible by a generous contribution from the MATRIX: MIDLAND Festival of the Midland Center for the Arts, Inc., Midland, Michigan, in recognition of the outstanding artistry of sculptor Marshall M. Fredericks. Additional funding provided by the Rosalind C. Fredericks Educational Trust and the Marshall M. Fredericks Foundation.

Book design by William A. Bostick
Book layout and production: Michael Savitski
Manuscript editor: Cynthia Newman Bohn
Printer: University Lithoprinters, Inc.

Distributed by Wayne State University Press, Detroit, Michigan, 48201

ISBN 0-9726929-0-8

Library of Congress Control Number 2003100074

Editor's Note

Edgar P. Richardson's essay was written when Marshall Fredericks was still living and was unrevised at the time of Richardson's own death in 1985. To avoid confusion, the present tense in which he wrote has been changed to past.

In the captions, unless otherwise noted, the single dimension given refers to height; when two dimensions are given, height precedes length or width. The name of the Marshall M. Fredericks Sculpture Museum at Saginaw Valley State University in University Center, Michigan, is abbreviated MFSM. The locations for objects in the photographs have been identified to the best of the authors' knowledge, except for that of Plasteline models, which would have been destroyed in the sculpture process. The preferred title for a work is listed first, with any alternate title in parentheses.

Frontispiece: Marshall M. Fredericks in his studio in Royal Oak, Michigan, c. 1970.

Endpapers: Based on a photograph by Maurice Hartwick.

Printed in the United States of America.

To My Family and My Friends

— Marshall Maynard Fredericks 1991

In memory of Rosalind and Marshall Fredericks

— Suki 2003

Credo

To me, Sculpture is a wonderful and exciting thing, vital and all absorbing. It is sometimes very discouraging and difficult but often, too, unbelievably gratifying and satisfying.

There are several things concerning Sculpture that I believe are extremely important. It must be wholly consistent and in harmony with the Architecture involved, as well as being a beautiful entity within itself. It must embody a significance suitable to and expressive of the purpose and setting, and finally it must have a constructive meaning for others.

I love people, for I have learned through many experiences, both happy and sad, how beautiful and wonderful they can be; therefore I want more than anything in the world to do Sculpture which will have real meaning for other people, many people, and might in some way encourage, inspire or give them happiness.

Marshall M. Fredericks, 1956

Contents

Foreword

Sculpture in public places has been a fixture of the human condition since the Colossus of Rhodes was one of the seven Wonders of the World and surely long before that as well. It enlivens our perception of our surroundings, reminds us of important human messages and, frequently, relieves an otherwise boring vista. To be sure there are also those examples where an otherwise brilliant vista is ruined by some hack, but such an instance is not germane here. Michigan, until recent years, took public sculpture seriously enough to have a formal commission on the subject, but that, along with other victims, fell by the fiscal wayside at the hands of governmental bean-counters who know the price of everything and the value of nothing.

Marshall Fredericks surely knew value when he saw it and, over a long and productive lifetime, added greatly to our public weal. Detroit alone is forever in his debt for providing an enduring symbol of its "spirit," that ever-elusive, ever Phoenix-like essence that defines the faith and self-worth of a great city.

Fredericks's work is, of course, both public and private, and his scale is from small to Herculean. But one imagines that every piece was, in his fondest dreams, destined to be expanded to its fullest potential and placed for all to enjoy, even though enjoyment in the privacy of one's home was surely acceptable. Coming as he did from a background that valued the works of Paul Manship, Gustav Vigeland, Bertel Thorvaldsen, and Carl Milles, is it any wonder that his oeuvre took the path it did.

His gentle vision belied the vast physical labor inherent in his work and his hours of patient finishing yielded a surface as pleasing to the eye as it was rewarding to the heart. His aim was to greet and seduce the visitor with his subject, and whether it was a green marble frog or a fifty-five-foot-tall cross, a gilt-bronze mouse, or a fountain that took nineteen years to complete—all were imagined with an enormous audience in mind, an audience that would return over and over to partake of the pleasure intended for them.

This work compiles a seventy-year career into a portable gazetteer, a guide to works of genius dispersed throughout the land, revered still by viewers whether they see the work for the first time or the fiftieth. Articles herein explore the man, his work, and his legacy. The museum devoted to his oeuvre stands as a monument of its own to a man who pleased so many.

"Tak," Marshall!

Samuel Sachs II
Director
The Frick Collection, New York

Acknowledgments

My father and William Bostick, with the support of Richard Kinney at Wayne State University Press, created a vision for this book over twenty-five years ago. Because of my father's full-time devotion to sculpting, the book was never completed in his lifetime, although he, Richard, and Bill determined the overall specifications, and the layout was essentially completed up through the pre-war years. Because of Bill's perseverance, patience, and enthusiasm, the creative life force of the book has been sustained and has now been fully realized. My siblings and I are deeply grateful to him for his incredible generosity with his time and design talents. We were fortunate that Mike Savitski agreed to complete the design work in keeping with Bill's vision. Mike also took on the enormous task of seeing the book through all the production phases up through publication.

I am thankful that we have been able to use Edgar Richardson's insightful introduction, written in 1981, with input from my father. I would also like to express my appreciation to the other major contributors, Sam Sachs, MaryAnn Wilkinson, Mino Duffy, Barbara Heller, Robin Salmon, and above all, Marcy Fisher, who, based on their personal experiences with my father and their professional thoroughness, intelligence, and sensitivity, collectively actualized the completion of the book. Marcy's enthusiasm for detail and accuracy in the compilation of the appendixes and captions, and in the preparation of the manuscript resulted in a comprehensive text that will provide a wealth of information to a variety of readers. We were blessed to have connected with Cynthia Newman Bohn, who as copy editor summa cum laude pulled together a multitude of voices, diplomatically taking into account my comments and those of the peer readers, and sensitively integrated them into a cohesive publication.

Alice Nigoghosian and Arthur Evans of Wayne State University Press supportively took the book through its initial stages of development. I owe particular thanks to Alice, for her sensible and diplomatic editorial advice, and am indebted to her for her continued support, which included generously guiding this project into the hands of Mike Savitski and Cindy Bohn, as well as facilitating the book's marketing and distribution through the press.

Many thanks go to all the other individuals and institutions who offered information, research materials, photographic resources, and technical assistance, including Susan Ballesteros and Betty Davis at the Detroit Institute of Arts, Joseph Becherer at Frederik Meijer Gardens and Sculpture Park, Mark Coir and Amy James at the Cranbrook Archives, Patty Delahanty and Gwen Pier at the National Sculpture Society, Christine Edmonson, Kristin Martin, and Monica Wolf at the Cleveland Museum of Art, Debra Polich at Artrain, as well as M. J. Davis, Rob Fisher, Ruth Graham, George Gurney, Dana Hartwick, James Maroney, Bonny McLaughlin, Dennis Nawrocki, Patricia Reed, and Roberta Starkweather, to name only a few. I greatly appreciate Molly Barth, Rita Copenhagen, and Scott Slocum for their contributions as my father's assistants; without them his later work would never have been accomplished. I also appreciate their involvement in this project and their superb memories. Furthermore, I am indebted to Pam Pangborn, who tirelessly supported Marcy and me with technical and research assistance, as well as the task of photo preparation and permissions.

Particular gratitude goes to Honey Arbury, who, with her husband Ned, made possible the Marshall Fredericks Sculpture Museum at Saginaw Valley State University, which was a dream come true for my father and is a gift to all who visit it. Further thanks go to Don Bachand, Chuck Graham, Jim Muladore, Michael Panhorst, Charlene Rathburn, Kathleen Theiler, and the board of the museum for facilitating the use of archival material, as well as attending to some of the financial and legal details of the project, with particular appreciation to Andrea Ondish for all her enthusiastic assistance. A special mention goes to Lyla Williams and Ginny Morrison, who got the ball rolling, along with Ted Giatas, former director of the Midland Center for the Arts, for Matrix Midland's generous financial contribution in support of this publication. And a big thank you to Michael Tiknis, current director of the center, David Wirth, and Bill Collins for implementing this commitment.

I would also like to thank my husband and children, who lovingly supported me during my work on the book, my siblings, who shared the commitment to complete this project, and to posthumously thank our mother, who not only spent many selfless hours on the book, and on documenting our father's work and activities over the years, but was his absolute mainstay in life.

Suki Fredericks

Marshall M. Fredericks, Sculptor

Marshall Fredericks was primarily active (although not exclusively) as a maker of public sculpture. Both in form and content public sculpture has requirements that differentiate it from either studio sculpture or ornament.

Public sculpture, whether designed as an enrichment of architecture or as freestanding monument, is made normally for open air, to be seen under constantly changing angles of sunlight, at varying distances, and in all weathers. Sunlight, far stronger than indoor light, demands firm, robust forms. The subtle nuances of surface possible in indoor sculpture are lost under the light of the sky. Fredericks himself spoke of natural light as "the most revealing light, demanding great perfection and strength of form and in the relationship and connection of forms."

Public sculpture differs from studio sculpture in content. When applied to architecture, it speaks to the passerby of the purpose of the building, as do the façade sculptures of Amiens or those of a baroque church. Standing alone, as a monument, it speaks to the passerby of a person, a hero, a communal memory. Such works are not the private musings of a sculptor but embody a public idea, saying "Remember" or "Here."

Our century has added new problems for public sculpture to solve. The enormous scale of the skyscraper dwarfs the human being and creates unprecedented problems of scale. The massive rectangularity of concrete and steel construction offers only a rigid grid of horizontals and verticals, and often quite meager entrances. The automobile hurtles its passengers at fifty or more miles an hour past a monument, which in another century addressed itself to the inspection of the foot passenger. The anonymous character of modern corporate institutions—a university administration building or a city hospital—makes their identities difficult to grasp or personify. Fredericks dealt with all of these problems.

Marshall Maynard Fredericks was born January 31, 1908, in Rock Island, Illinois. He received his early training in sculpture at John Huntington Polytechnic Institute and the Cleveland School of Art, both in Cleveland, Ohio. Working during summers for his father, who was in the construction business, he received valuable experience in the nature and finishing of materials and in the moving, shipping, and erecting of heavy objects. In 1930, at age twenty-two, he received the Herman Matzen Traveling Scholarship in Sculpture from the Cleveland School of Art and was able to go to Europe. He sought out sculptor Carl Milles in Sweden, drawn by admiration for his bronze fountain figures. Milles liked the young American of Scandinavian ancestry and gave him work among the stone carvers in the studio. He became a very skillful stone carver. Throughout his career he turned to stone carving in both public and private pieces, showing great finish and perfection in his use of the material.[1]

After a time Milles sent Fredericks to Munich to gain experience at two renowned schools of the day, the Heimann Schule and the Schwegerle Schule. Fredericks worked also at the Académie Scandinav in Paris and wandered about Europe, looking at things in Copenhagen, Rome, London, as art students do. By the time he returned to America, Milles had come to the United States to work at Cranbrook and was in need of an assistant who knew the mechanics of large-scale sculpture. He asked Fredericks to help him both in teaching and as an assistant in the studio. Fredericks remained at Cranbrook nine and a half years.

Cranbrook

Cranbrook, situated in the rolling morainic landscape north of Detroit, Michigan, was a project of George G. Booth, publisher of the *Detroit News*. Deeply interested in the Arts and Crafts movement, in the early 1920s Booth set out to create an art and educational village. He built first a village church in the Gothic style, designed by Bertram G. Goodhue Associates, whose interior was enriched by work of the leading artisans in the Arts and Crafts movement at that time. A change of direction came in 1927 when Booth brought the Finnish architect Eliel Saarinen to Cranbrook as architect-in-residence. Saarinen built an ensemble of buildings, a school for boys, another for girls, a museum of art, a museum of science, an art school, studios, and residences. He gathered about him a group of highly talented Swedish craftsmen and Carl Milles, a sculptor of major reputation in Europe as a creator of outdoor bronze figures and fountains, as sculptor-in-residence. Fredericks could not have found a better place to learn how to master the problems of monumental sculpture in bronze.

The Approach to Outdoor Sculpture

Fredericks's first works, such as the busts *Russell Barnett Aitken* (fig. 2) and *Portrait of a Japanese (Nobuji Yoshida)* (fig. 13) and *Polo Player* (fig. 18), are those of a young and talented sculptor working in the scale and complex surfaces of indoor sculpture. An early outdoor work provides evidence that Fredericks felt a sculptor's interest in the block/mass form popular in the sculpture of the 1930s but gave it his individual touch. In front of both the Detroit Institute of Arts and Cleveland Museum of Art broods Auguste Rodin's bronze *Thinker.* When the Cranbrook Art Museum was completed, George Booth said to Fredericks, "Marshall, I want you to do a *Thinker* to put on the steps of the Cranbrook museum. Every museum has a *Thinker* in front. We should have one." To do Rodin's sculpture over again in any form was unthinkable. With the shrewd humor he sometimes exhibited, Fredericks chose a block of black granite and carved the massive, self-enclosed ape that now sits before the Cranbrook Art Museum (fig. 56). When it was shown to him, Booth looked at it for a moment disconcerted; then recognizing the idea and the sculpture's quality, he said, "Well, it may be that he is thinking far more interesting thoughts than we are. I'll take it."

The commission that started Fredericks on his real career came when he won a national competition for the design of a fountain to be erected on Belle Isle, a city of Detroit park on an island in the river between the United States and Canada. The central figure of the *Levi L. Barbour Memorial Fountain* (figs. 32–33, pl. 9) is a leaping gazelle, in bronze on a granite pedestal, the whole sixteen feet high, rising from a basin into which jets of water fall, forming a circular screen of water. A circular wall of verdure surrounds the fountain; its four entrances or axes are marked by four small carved granite beasts and birds positioned in the falling water. The clear, strong silhouette of the gazelle, the stylized modeling of the smaller animals, and the appeal of the animal subject to visitors of every age combined to form the happy debut of a monumental sculptor.

In 1940–42 Fredericks executed one of the most graceful and winning of his early works, the *Two Sisters* fountain, which was cast and erected, after the interruption of World War II, in 1964 in a courtyard of Kingswood School for Girls at Cranbrook (figs. 94–96 and 300). The evolution of his style gave to these human figures also the clarity of silhouette, the clean, firm forms, and the stylized detail required for a piece in sunlight.

Architectural Sculpture

Fresh and original, the two fountains are nevertheless within the realm of what Fredericks learned from Milles. The next step was to take him completely out of Milles's orbit.

One of the casualties of the Great Depression was architectural sculpture. It was as if a curtain came down after the completion of Rockefeller Center in New York. All the sculptural activity of the 1920s, good, bad, and indifferent—monuments in parks, on public buildings, in theatres and movie houses, even hotels—came suddenly to an end. Ironically, as architectural sculpture ceased, there followed a wave of mural painting, largely inspired by the Mexican mural movement of the 1920s. Two of Mexico's chief mural painters, Diego Rivera and José Clemente Orozco, came to work in the United States in the early 1930s, and in 1931 Rivera frescoed the inner court of the Detroit Institute of Arts. This was followed in 1932 by a commission in Rockefeller Center in New York City. The sensational controversies aroused by the frescoes in Detroit and New York proved of fleeting interest, yet Rivera had a strong influence upon the proliferation of wall painting under the Works Progress Administration (WPA) and Treasury Department programs in the arts. His work certainly strengthened, if it did not create, a new style of massive block-like treatment of the human figure, both in painting and sculpture; and he introduced into the subject matter of art the machines of modern technology.

Fredericks's First Architectural Commission—The Horace H. Rackham Educational Memorial Building

In 1939 the Engineering Society of Detroit was planning to build a headquarters on a city block facing a green park containing two white marble buildings, the Detroit Institute of Arts, designed by Paul Cret, and the Detroit Public Library, designed by Cass Gilbert. The plan was later enlarged to house as well the extension division in Detroit of the University of Michigan. The architects chosen were Harley, Ellington and Day, whose chief designer, Malcolm R. Stirton, was ambitious to make the building worthy of its site and, if possible, to use local talent. Fredericks had demonstrated in the Belle Isle fountain and at Cranbrook a monumental style in both bronze and stone. He was selected as sculptor and was brought in at the beginning of the planning. Stirton filled a city block with a long, freestanding white marble structure with four façades (fig. 87). Its long main façade faces north, the east and west façades are short; what was a south façade is now concealed by a parking garage. On these Fredericks created some forty-six reliefs telling the story of the building's varied functions of science, engineering, and education. The center of the main façade is occupied by the bowed front of an auditorium, while the Engineering Society in the east wing and the University Extension in the west each have their own entrance, and the latter has a secondary door in the short western wall. Fredericks designed enrichment for all the key points—the pylons of the auditorium front and the entrances on the north, south, east, and west fronts (figs. 87–93). In subject these carved reliefs are drawn from contemporary life, stylized and given monumental treatment. One science, Astronomy, has an historical subject: an ancient Chinese astronomer making the earliest recorded observation of an eclipse of the sun (fig. 90). In the others an airplane, a dynamo, a microscope, a school desk are symbols drawn directly from the world about us. The battle to make technology and engineering acceptable subjects in art had been fought over Rivera's frescoes in the Detroit Institute of Arts, and won. Fredericks was free to choose his subjects in contemporary America and to develop them into parts of the rhythm of the architecture.

The sculptures of the Rackham Building are a landmark in Fredericks's development; as the building itself was in the fortunes of the architectural firm of Harley, Ellington and Day, giving the firm a high reputation as creators of one of Detroit's admired monuments.

The New York World's Fair Fountain

Asked to do a fountain for the Glass Industries Building at the New York World's Fair of 1939, Fredericks returned to the universal appeal of animals for his subject, but he gave the fountain an ingenious reversal of the common pattern of high centerpiece and water playing to the outward rim. He designed a ring of monumental baboon figures, in cast stone, fourteen feet high with their pedestals, with a baby baboon sitting in the middle of an eight-foot glass basin, into which the jets of water play from the outer circumference (fig. 82). This fountain no longer exists; during the war, when the site was acquired for the war effort by the Army Corps of Engineers, it was stolen and is thought to have been dumped into the East River.

World War II and Marriage

World War II took Fredericks into the Army Air Corps. He served in South Asia, rising to the rank of lieutenant colonel. It also brought him a fortunate marriage to Rosalind Bell Cooke, of Grosse Pointe, Michigan, who gave him a happy personal life and an able, intelligent aide in the management of his career. The first two of their five children, twin sons, were born while he was in India.

On the way home from the war, he received the news, in Chicago, that he had been commissioned to execute a war memorial fountain for the city of Cleveland. Little did he know that nineteen years of study and development would go into that work, which was not put into place until 1964.

Experiments in Materials and Forms

Fredericks was always open to experimenting with new forms and new materials: the medallion portrait used as a memorial, as in the *George Gough Booth and Ellen Scripps Booth Memorial* at Cranbrook (fig. 150) and the *Willard Henry Dow* plaque in memory of the son of the founder of the Dow Chemical Company; the relief-like row of stylized figures called *Saints and Sinners* (figs. 71 and 316); studies of animals and human figures in polished vari-colored granites and in polished bronze. During this period, he developed his use of the natural colors of stone or metal; and gave them luster by polishing.

The Veterans Memorial Building, Detroit[2]

The city of Detroit faces a river, which is more truly a deep and swift-flowing strait a mile wide, through which passes an impressive parade of ships. By 1950 the waterfront had grown into a confused array of railroad yards, wharves, and factories, many of which had fallen into decay. After the war the city determined to reclaim the waterfront for civic use. Harley, Ellington and Day, with the prestige of the Rackham Building behind them, were commissioned to start the revival of the waterfront with a Veterans Memorial Building, and Malcolm Stirton as chief designer again brought Fredericks in to collaborate on the design.

The Veterans Memorial forms a long rectangle of white marble. One short end, with a glass-enclosed terrace at the top, looks across the river to Canada. The other faces Jefferson Avenue, the oldest road in Michigan, running parallel to the river and now carrying a great stream of automobile traffic. The sculptural enrichment of this face was the subject of much study. Fredericks's suggestion was ultimately adopted; to make this wall without windows so that the entire end of the building should count as a single monument, whose one feature is a giant relief of an eagle, thirty feet high and projecting boldly from the wall. The V of its wings symbolizes victory; in its talons it bears the laurel and palm, symbols of glory and of victory (fig. 135, pl. 10). As the pedestrian approaches the entrance, marked by a red granite wall on which is Fredericks's rendition of the Great Seal of the United States in polished bronze, he passes seven marble pylons, each carved with an historical subject in incised low relief (figs. 140–144). The design is thus on two scales. The eagle speaks to those passing on the highway; the seven pylons and the entrance sculpture are scaled to those approaching on foot.

At a later date (and without consulting the sculptor) the pylons were moved to another alignment and, worse still, their delicate reliefs blurred by sandblasting.[3]

The Louisville Courier Journal Building

The main entrance to the building of the Louisville *Courier-Journal* presented another kind of problem—to embody the spirit and the history of a state in visual form. The building was a not unusual downtown business structure, having an entrance in the form of a shallow rectangular recess. Fredericks took as the subject for its enrichment the history of the region, in which the *Courier-Journal* is the one great newspaper. Kentucky, one of the earliest states to be settled by the tide of western migration, has a store of memories: the pioneer settlers, the great rivers with their picturesque side-wheelers, its farms and blooded horses. The tall space over the door was a difficulty which was solved by grouping these memories in bronze low reliefs, arranged as if free-flowing on a polished black granite background, as they might present themselves in the imagination—a pioneer family with the animals in the forest; riverboats and giant catfish; tobacco and sheep; thoroughbred horses. These free-form reliefs, completed in 1948, were a skillful solution to the problem of an awkwardly shaped wall area (fig. 116).

The Eaton War Memorial

Free-form reliefs in metal upon a contrasting stone background, as seen in the Louisville doorway, were a favorite device of Fredericks's to enrich the flat planes and austere surfaces of twentieth-century architecture. He used it in a variety of places to express a variety of themes.

The War Memorial (1948) for the Eaton Manufacturing Corporation of Cleveland, Ohio, is an instance of its use in an interior space, where the sculpture and the list of names are to be seen at close range and the scale is necessarily small (fig. 123). In other instances it is used on a very large scale.

The Administration Building, University of Michigan [4]

The Administration Building of the University of Michigan, designed by Harley, Ellington and Day and completed in 1949, is another instance of the collaboration of Malcolm Stirton as architect and Marshall Fredericks as sculptor. The building's design is one of sober and impressive dignity. Its main entrance is marked by a massive tower rising through the façade, whose vertical thrust is emphasized by the tiers of windows. On either side long, unbroken bands of windows, with rather delicately molded trim, give a strong horizontal emphasis. The effect of dignity and severe rectangularity is relieved by Fredericks's sculpture, which is ingeniously but sparingly placed and enlivened by humor. On the dark stone panels at the floor levels of the tower windows are hammered aluminum reliefs of stylized plant forms, which add a flicker of light, and shadow-like floral crockets on a Gothic framework (fig. 125). At the main door the entrant is greeted by two reliefs, *The Dream of the Young Girl* (husband, children, home) and *The Dream of the Young Man* (wandering and adventure), free-floating forms on two walls (fig. 127).

In the rear the horizontal bands of window, brick, and masonry are interrupted at ground level by a porch, and at the second level by two limestone reliefs set as accents, *Aesop*, representing the European background of our culture, and *Hiawatha*, representing the American (fig. 128). On the black band of stone over the porch are three-foot-long free-form aluminum reliefs, and over the doors into the wings are reliefs in limestone of a young girl with a rabbit and birds (*Naturalist*) (fig. 129); baboons playing musical instruments (*Musicians*); and baboons peering into books and looking though a magnifying glass (*Scientists*) (fig. 134). These embellishments, nicely placed and pleasing in a variety of forms and materials, are both thoughtful and amusing.

What is notable in these buildings is the harmony of architectural mass and its sculptural enrichment—both in contemporary idiom—and the freshness of the symbolism. Fredericks seems to have escaped (if that is the proper word) easily from the old classical imagery of Greece and Rome, worn smooth by centuries of use, embracing instead images of the wilderness, the Indian, the pioneer, the modern life of America. Perhaps this came to him naturally. To a thoughtful boy growing up in Rock Island, Illinois, on the Mississippi, early in our century, the Indian and pioneer past was still near and vivid. Although Iroquois and Cherokee still live in the eastern states—and the music of Indian names is everywhere—on the eastern coast the pioneer stage is overlain by many other memories. It seems closer on the Mississippi. As Carl Sandburg wrote in his poem "Chicago" in *Slabs of the Sunburnt West*:

It is easy for a child to get breakfast and push off
to school with a pair of roller skates,
buns for lunch, and a geography,
Riding through the tunnel under a river running backward
to school to listen . . . how the Pottawatomies
and the Blackhawks . . . ran on moccasins . . .
between Kaskaskia, Peoria, Kankakee and Chicago

Union Station, Detroit

Union Station on Fort Street in Detroit was a landmark of nineteenth-century Romanesque architecture used by the Chesapeake and Ohio, Baltimore and Ohio, Pennsylvania, and Wabash railroads. Passengers left from its platforms for the great ports of the Atlantic coast south of New York, and for St. Louis and the West. When it was remodeled and modernized after the war, Fredericks was asked to do something on the long narrow band of wall over the doors through which travelers passed to the train platforms. On what would appear an awkwardly long and constricted span, Fredericks executed in polished aluminum a free-floating relief, forty-four feet long, which he called *The Romance of Transportation* (figs. 151–154). Beginning at the left with the opening of the West—Indians, a wagon train, stagecoaches, highwaymen— the relief swells into a crescendo of railroads and a streamlined train, then tapers off through airplanes and automobiles, to motorcycles and bicycles. The successive forms flow into each other, accentuated by the gleam of hammered and polished aluminum, leading the eye easily from one end to the other of a symbolic history of a people in movement. The relief was put in place in 1951. Subsequently, as the railroads' passenger traffic declined, the Fort Street Station, as it was popularly known, was demolished. The relief was removed to the Railroad Museum in Baltimore, where it remains on view.

The War Memorial in the United States

The war memorial as an expression of proud and tragic memories came into prominence as a theme of sculpture after the Civil War. Often that tragedy was represented in terms of the individual soldier—the bronze infantryman quietly standing guard—an image which spoke so eloquently to our country that it was repeated in a thousand towns and villages. In more heroic form, the Civil War was commemorated by a general on horseback, as if at the head of his volunteer soldiers. In the vast wars of our century the individual was submerged and generals no longer rode at the head of their troops. Memories of those who served were commemorated impersonally by a flame, a sports stadium, a civic auditorium. Fredericks planned one such dramatic, impersonal commemoration of Bataan, (fig. 114), but it was never executed.

When asked to do a war memorial for the University of Michigan in 1950, he turned again to the symbolic eagle, which he had used in the Veterans Memorial Building in Detroit. The *American Eagle* in Ann Arbor is a fierce, combative image of courage and strength (fig. 148). A heroic bronze, poised on its pedestal, it shows how far he had come in expressive power from the simple grace of his early fountain figures. The observer who walks around this bronze sees a continuously changing, merging series of views, the work maintaining its vigor and meaning throughout. This is not a one- or four-sided composition but a kinetic, continuously unfolding design.

The Ohio Union, Ohio State University, Columbus

The problem of a continuously unfolding series of views came to a different solution in Fredericks's treatment, in 1951, of an austere monumental structure, the Ohio Union (Student Union) in Columbus. The pedestrian approaching the Union walks parallel to a plain limestone wall at a distance of about ten feet. To enrich this long, unbroken plane with sunlight and shadow, Fredericks carved six bold, eight-foot-tall reliefs intended to catch the eye in succession. Once again he made use of the memories of the region—the Indians and the wild creatures of the forest; Johnny Appleseed; pioneers and early settlers; freighters on the rivers; the steel industry; farmers, potters, pioneers of aircraft; figures from government and education (figs. 161–166). The reliefs offer a rich play of light and shadow and a thoughtful evocation of the state from which the student body comes.

No task is more difficult than to abandon a long-established, successful set of symbolic forms and find new ones. One can see this in the art of architecture. Confronted by the colossal buildings of the twentieth century, architects tried first to adapt classical columns and the acanthus leaf to a new scale, then to invent a new Art Deco vocabulary of streamlined orna-ment, and finally dispensed with enrichment altogether. One may imagine the difficulties for a sculptor of forsaking the gods of Olympus and creating a new vocabulary drawn from everyday life, the memories, the work, the tools of today. It is one of Fredericks's achievements that he used our own world as subject matter, symbolically presented but nonetheless the familiar stuff of American life.

The Ford Rotunda

In the instance of the Ford Rotunda, Fredericks's problem was a circular wall high over the heads of the visitors. The Rotunda was erected originally to house the Ford Motor Company's exhibit at the Chicago World's Fair of 1932–33. It was re-erected at Dearborn as a reception center for visitors to the Ford plant and, although intended to be permanent, was lightly con-structed. Closed during World War II, it reopened in 1953, and was destroyed by fire nine years later.

Fredericks's sixteen free-form reliefs, representing the materials and skills that go into the making of an automobile (figs. 172–177), were executed in fiberglass polyester resin laminate, which was well suited to the lightweight construction. The reliefs are so well matched in scale to their position that, although eight feet tall, they give no impression of being either large or small (figs. 178–180).

The City-County Building of Detroit [5]

In 1955, when a new building was to be erected to house city and county offices as a focal point of Detroit's new riverfront, the architects Harley, Ellington and Day again asked Fredericks's collaboration. It was an assignment to daunt the boldest sculptor. The twenty-story white marble building was to stand at the junction of two streets, Woodward and Jefferson Avenues, carrying heavy streams of automobile traffic. The building was to be a long rectangle, its nar-row western end facing the intersection of the oldest and most historic roads in the state.

Again, as in the Veterans Memorial Building, the narrow end of the building was treated as a single monument. At its base Fredericks designed a kneeling giant, in green bronze, five times life size, representing the *Spirit of Detroit* (fig. 230, pls. 14–15). In one outstretched hand the male figure holds a gilt-bronze sphere symbolizing the spirit of God or deity, in the other a gilt-bronze group of the human family. A marble screen behind the bronze figure forms a transition between the statue and the lofty wall behind; it also serves to conceal a building entrance that might otherwise seem a mere mouse hole. Building, screen, and statue form a harmonious whole.

The marble screen serves to identify the building through the official seals of Wayne County and the city of Detroit carved on its surface. Beneath the seals is an inscription: "Now the Lord is that Spirit and where the Spirit of the Lord is, there is Liberty (II Corinthians 3:17)."

As often happens, the best solution of a problem (and this one is very successful) is a simple one: A figure, both at rest and suggesting movement; familiar yet symbolizing the complexities of time, space and thought; heroic and accessible. Completed in 1958, the *Spirit of Detroit* was immediately popular, warmly embraced by both the public and the officials within the building. It was given an affectionate nickname, "The Jolly Green Giant," and used on official stationery as a logo and as a symbol of the city on billboards directing visitors approaching the city via major highways. Few sculptures have been so promptly adopted as the symbolic image of a city.

A Hospital and a Library

American architecture of the mid-twentieth century is rich in massive, unbroken wall surfaces; most of these are dignified but mute. Fredericks was singularly successful in transforming such walls by creating a free-form relief in metal, placing it with a most sensitive eye for its decorative effect, and making a silent wall speak of the nature of the building.

In 1955 on such a wall of the Beaumont Memorial Hospital in Royal Oak, Michigan, Fredericks executed an aluminum group, *The Family Protected by Healing Herbs*. Dignified, elegantly decorative, and appealing in its sentiment, it, too, has been adopted by the hospital as its logo or emblem (fig. 199).

For a similar great, plain wall at the New Dallas Public Library of Dallas, Texas, he executed an aluminum relief, *Youth in the Hands of God*, again, placed with exquisite precision to enhance the wall. So well fitted is this work to its wall that one is unconscious of size; although twenty feet high, it belongs quite naturally to the place it occupies (fig. 216).[6]

The Henry and Edsel Ford Auditorium, Detroit

The climax of Fredericks's achievement in the free-form relief is, unlike the works described previously, indoors and designed to be seen by artificial light in the Ford Auditorium, which was built in 1955–56 to house the Detroit Symphony Orchestra and be the centerpiece of the city's new waterfront. The auditorium was a gift to Detroit, in memory of Henry and Edsel Ford, from Ford Motor Company dealers throughout the nation. The architects, Odell, Hewlett and Luckenbach, provided a deep, enclosed lobby, where in inclement weather people could remove their wraps or stamp snow from their feet. Beyond this is a long, curved foyer, at each end of which stairs ascend to a balcony giving access to the upper-level seats at the rear of the concert hall. This foyer offered the sculptor three large walls. One sweeps across the entire width of the hall above the entrance doors. At either end are tall walls above the staircases. The subject chosen by the sculptor for the long wall over the entrance doors was the Ford empire—not in pride or triumph—but in celebration of the infinitely complex elements of nature and human skills that were brought together to form the worldwide business.

A huge sculptural mural of colored metal, 145 feet long, fabricated of brass and aluminum, sweeps across the long, curved wall (fig. 212, pl. 12). The things of nature at one end and the qualities of man at the other flow together into the central image. Sculpture cannot be as ethereal as music, but like music these open-work forms suggest rather than define. Suspended about three inches off the wall, a web of white and gold metal rods gleams softly in the light—a truly remarkable imaginative image. Innovative also was the work's construction; its huge gleaming web is held together by thousands of welded joints. It seems to float there weightless, a spectacular celebration of a city and industry forged of metal.

On the end walls above the stairs the mood changes. Circus figures and harlequins, of repoussé brass and copper plated with cadmium, zinc, and gold, glitter and shine in a playful contrast to the shimmering mystery of the great relief (fig. 210, pl. 13).[7]

The Henry J. McMorran Auditorium, Port Huron, Michigan

The McMorran Auditorium is a memorial to a man whose most distinctive trait was a passion for exactness and precision of time. To celebrate this characteristic Fredericks designed a clock that is an intricately decorative web of gold anodized aluminum, twenty feet in diameter, which is lighted from within at night. The passing of time has seldom been so richly celebrated in any

American city as by the tracery of leaves and flowers forming the face of this clock and by the planets around it on the face of architect Alden Dow's monumental wall. At the time of its completion in 1962, the rich, inventive clock face was the first use of anodized aluminum in sculpture of any large dimension (fig. 255).

Beneath the clock is a pool and fountain in which two bronze figures, *Day* and *Night*, male and female, sweep in silent flight toward unknown ends (fig. 248, pl. 17).

A Variety of Other Work

Architectural sculpture is perhaps what is chiefly outstanding in Fredericks's work. Each building he enriched became an identifiable entity among the anonymous colossi that form our modern cities. This is achievement enough; but he created a variety of other works, large and small, grave and gay: medals, medallions, portraits, sculpture for children, sculpture of and for animals, memorials to memorable men.

Fond of children, he created animal figures that look like enlarged children's toys (figs. 184, 222, 295, 309, and 331, pl. 30) on which children can play when they come with their parents to suburban shopping centers. Sympathetic to animals, in 1955 he made for the cages of the great apes in the Detroit Zoo a series of strong, brightly colored shapes on which the apes can climb and perch (figs. 186–187, pl. 11). This humorous and playful element is prominent in his work. There is also a deeply reflective side.

The Indian River Shrine

At Indian River in northern Michigan, there is a beautiful but very small chapel, designed by the architect Alden Dow. In 1952 the priest at the chapel asked Fredericks to design an outdoor crucifix. The result, completed in 1959, was a huge bronze figure of Christ, twenty-eight feet high and twenty feet across the arms, hanging on a fifty-five-foot-tall redwood cross (fig. 238). The emphasis upon blood and agony in many crucifixes was repugnant to the sculptor. The priest obtained permission from Rome to eliminate these and Fredericks created a crucified figure of only sadness and resignation. The enormous size and solemnity of the figure have created a focus for pilgrimage, a crucifix of tragic and heroic grandeur, deep in the evergreen forest (pl. 16).

Macauley, Holden, and Ford Memorials

Alvan Macauley, president of the Packard Motor Company and longtime president of the Automobile Manufacturers Association, was one of the most respected men in the city of Detroit. To mark his grave in Elmwood Cemetery in 1955 Fredericks created a bronze group on a pedestal of dark green Norwegian granite; two wild geese rise in flight together, silently evoking memory and hope (fig. 207). In the imagery of American memorials, this is new and touching.

Created four years later in 1960, the memorial to James B. Holden, a man of great modesty, integrity, and generosity, is in quite a different mood. An annual New Year's reception given by him at the Detroit Club was an occasion that brought all elements of the city together. Among his many interests the Detroit Zoo was perhaps his favorite. Before the entrance to the Holden Museum of Living Reptiles stands a slender granite pedestal on which Fredericks placed a pair of bronze pterodactyls, locked in flying combat. It is a dramatic and sinister image which Holden would, in life, have greatly enjoyed (figs. 240–241).

A statue in memory of Henry Ford, intended for the grounds of the Henry Ford Centennial Library in Dearborn and completed in 1975, presented a quite different problem. A statue on an open sweep of lawn required a background of some sort. The man himself was both an ordinary country-born American and a genius, both an unassuming businessman and a man of pronounced individuality. Fredericks set himself the task of perpetuating exactly what the man was and how he looked. After studying hundreds of photographs, Fredericks created a wholly convincing image—to anyone who has seen the living Henry Ford, this is what he was. To create a background where none was to be found, and to say a little of what made this ordinary man in a business suit into a personality of worldwide fame, he added a dark green marble screen behind the bronze figure. On it are bronze reliefs of the automobile, the great factories, the farm machines, the epic transformation of rural life—a three-dimensional storybook of a memorable life (fig. 315).

The Final Development of the Freestanding Group

The historic development of sculpture from a niche figure offering a single principal view to the freestanding statue took place in Italy in the fifteenth and sixteenth centuries. In that evolution the freestanding figure was developed into a composition offering four principal views. In his *Autobiography* Florentine sculptor Benvenuto Cellini praised the discernment of Duke Cosimo de' Medici, who, on first seeing Cellini's *Neptune Fountain* "walked all around it stopping at each of the four points of view exactly as the ripest experts would have done." This was the basis for centuries of development of the freestanding monument. One step remained, the helical composition, in which as one walks around it a succession of perspectives flow one into another, making a sculpture interesting from every point of view.

The Expanding Universe and Freedom of the Human Spirit

In 1964 Fredericks executed for the inner court of the State Department Building in Washington, D.C., a fountain called *The Expanding Universe.* A star-crowned figure in bronze and nickel crouches on a globe, around which whirls a shining orbit. There are smaller orbits in each of the figure's outstretched hands. The colors and reflections of bronze, nickel, and splashing water are used with vigor and subtlety. The figure, seen from any point, is almost of equal interest on every side (fig. 263, pl. 18).

In Flushing, New York, on the grounds of the old site of the United Nations, a composition of two figures and two wild swans rising upward in free flight, was erected in the same year. Commissioned for the United States Pavilion at the World's Fair, *Freedom of the Human Spirit* (fig. 273, pl. 22), twenty-seven feet high, is a striking achievement of poetic movement—a goal Fredericks had pursued from his earliest works.[8]

The Cleveland War Memorial

In 1964, almost two decades after it was first commissioned and following years of study and preparation, Fredericks brought to fruition what stands as the pinnacle of his work with freestanding groups. The War Memorial fountain in Cleveland, Ohio, was to be placed in a long quadrangle of park formed by rectangular blocks of public buildings. At one end of the park is an office tower, at the other a sports stadium. Fredericks made many studies, building a scale model of the entire architectural complex, to determine the best spot for the fountain, how it was to be best lighted at night, trying various compositions for the central figures. In the center of the work soaring upward movement symbolizes eternal life, the universal human hope/dream/religious faith, which springs up everywhere in the human heart. His initial concept, two figures side by side, grew finally into a single figure soaring out of flame-like forms rising from the earth (figs. 274, 278). Below the central helical shaft of forty-six-foot-high rising forms are four massive blocks of dark green granite set in the fountain's pool. In their intricate carvings the eye discerns the four quarters of the earth, in representing the idea that all peoples and civilizations recognize man's immortal spirit (figs. 285–288). A sphere, filigreed in its entirety and illuminated from within, supports the central figure. Around it streams the river of life, bearing with it animals, plants, birds, the shining sun. A universal ideal is given an expression neither obvious, not liturgical, calling upon the spectator to study and reflect (fig. 289, pls. 19–20).

Throughout his career Fredericks worked by himself, apart from the world of designers, avant-garde critics, curators, and academics. He worked instead with architects, civic committees, contractors, masons, bronze casters, businessmen, Americans of every sort in the active stream of life. In dealing with them he had a secret weapon, of which I believe he was never aware—his mind worked naturally in harmony with theirs. He dealt with ideas comprehensible to the American people: the family, American history, animals, children, human works and skills, universal emotions and aspirations. As he himself said of his work:

> There are several things concerning sculpture that I believe are extremely important. It must be wholly consistent and in harmony with the architecture involved, as well as being a beautiful entity within itself. It must embody significance suitable to and expressive of the purpose and setting, and finally it must have a constructive meaning for others. I love people, for I have learned through many experiences, both happy and sad, how beautiful and wonderful they can be; therefore, I want more than anything in the world to do sculpture which will have real meaning for other people, many people, and might in some way encourage, inspire, or give them happiness.

Marshall Fredericks was a sculptor of great talents who was instinctively at one with his world.

E. P. Richardson
Philadelphia, 1981

1. Examples of his exceptional skill in stone carving are the *Torso of a Dancer* (fig. 52) in black Belgian marble and the *Moray Eel and Fish* in green granite (fig. 97), both in the Cranbrook Art Museum, and the *Siberian Ram* in limestone in front of the Baldwin Library, Birmingham, Michigan (fig. 258). Outstanding examples of the use of stone as part of a monument, both in imaginative concept and technical facility, are the four massive groups, in emerald-pearl granite, at the base of the Cleveland War Memorial Fountain (figs. 285–288). In fact, he seems to have been equally at home in either stone or metal (E. P. Richardson).
2. Currently named the UAW-Ford National Program Center.
3. The façade of the building was recently altered (windows added) when the building was renovated
4. Currently named the Literature, Science and Arts Building.
5. Currently named the Coleman A. Young Municipal Center.
6. The library was sold and the relief is now located at the Marshall M. Fredericks Sculpture Museum at Saginaw Valley State University.
7. The Ford Auditorium was closed in 1989; the future placement of the sculptures is yet to be determined.
8. A cast of this work is installed in Shain Park in Birmingham, Michigan.

An Expanding Universe: The Late Work of Marshall Fredericks

A
rt historians have posited that work created by an artist at the end of his career—the so-called late work—is often demonstrative of a change in direction or focus, a new emphasis on mortality, or an attempt to make up for lost time. The work of Marshall Fredericks's later years, however, has a remarkable consistency, solidity, and purposefulness that builds upon rather than departs from the foundation of his earlier work. He continued to make works based upon the themes that had always occupied him and to choose subjects that expressed his own version of humanism. His abstracted, often rather hard-edged style, with its Art Deco flavor, continued to appeal to him and to his public. Subtle variations on his signature style became more important in his last works, proof that his artistic vision and creativity remained vital. While Fredericks followed a different path from his contemporaries, who brought avant-garde ideas to the creation of sculpture, his sensitive integration of fine arts with design has had lasting public impact.

In the early years of the twentieth century, sculptors such as Constantin Brancusi and Pablo Picasso rejected classical ideals and moved instead toward the creation of a new set of artistic values for sculpture, including an embrace of the principles of cubism, the sensuality of the exotic and the primitive, and the machine aesthetic. Their search to create pure form by making a decisive break with the past came to typify modernism. Others, however, such as Swedish sculptor Carl Milles, schooled in the traditional sculptural values of his mentor, the French sculptor Auguste Rodin, continued the classical idiom well into the mid-twentieth-century. This approach relied upon a sensitivity to mass and volume, traditional materials such as bronze and stone, and, above all, figurative imagery used in either a narrative or an allegorical sense. The early influence of Milles and the Scandinavian version of modernism remained crucial to Fredericks's work throughout his career. Restrained, stylized forms and attenuated figure types are the hallmarks of their approach to modernism, an interpretation that borrowed liberally from the archaisms associated with Art Deco.

From his mentor Milles, Fredericks learned to conceive of sculpture as a corollary to architectural design that must of necessity take into account the building or site with which it is associated. Fredericks cultivated the ability to conceptualize sculpture not simply as mass but as an object that defines and is defined by space. This skill allowed him first to explore and then to exploit the complex interrelationships between his sculpture and the architecture that was to surround it. Fredericks's notion of what constitutes a monument is particularly important. For him, a monument was not simply sculpture on a large scale; works such as the *Ann Arbor War Memorial Eagle* (fig. 148). *Siberian Ram* (fig. 258), and *The Thinker* (fig. 56) retain their sense of mass and power even when reduced in size. His understanding of form and space allowed him to work successfully in a variety of sizes, from jewelry to gigantic fountains, while preserving his own unique blend of verve and dynamism.

In his fountain sculptures Fredericks successfully fused static and dynamic elements by exploring linear and liquid forms and by emphasizing large spatial areas to create overall patterns. Fredericks's great admiration for Milles is particularly apparent in *God on the Rainbow*, 1995 (fig. 342), a work he enlarged in tribute to the older artist and which is based on Milles's design.

Here, Fredericks invokes a classic Milles type for the figure, managing to keep him both slender and bulbous at the same time, in contrast to the more angular treatment that is typical of Fredericks's figures. The sense of scale, the open attitude of the figure, and the dynamic physicality of the pose clearly reflect Milles's style as a continuing influence in Fredericks's work. Here, too, the ability to sculpt with a moving medium finds expression in the use of water to complete the arch form. This "collaboration" confounds our understanding of the conventional attributes of solid and liquid, of static and moving shapes, of silence and sound.

Fredericks's ability to achieve a felicitous marriage of sculpture and architecture found its purest expression in his influence on the design for the Marshall M. Fredericks Sculpture Museum at Saginaw Valley State University. From the beginning, he collaborated with the architects, bringing a sculptor's eye to the relationships of space and scale inherent in the building. He was particularly interested in the placement of the works of art and the relationships of scale between the sculpture and the interior spaces. A modernistic, cubistic design reminiscent of Eliel Saarinen's Cranbrook Art Museum and Library, the building has a classical, logical balance that seems to derive legitimacy from its solid monumentality. The building's glass façade echoes the grand ceremonial propylaeum that connects the museum and library in Saarinen's antecedent, and a fountain and pool filled with lithe, angular figures graces the front of both.

Fredericks's skill in siting his sculpture was an important aspect of the museum project; other works were cast or installed after his death and thus did not have his direct input. He was able, however, to enlarge, oversee casting and site three important later works: *Wings of the Morning* (designed in 1969, fig. 302), which he placed at Brookgreen Gardens in 1986 (pl. 25) and also at Kirk in the Hills (fig. 319); *The Clowns* (designed in 1937, figs. 43–44) placed at the Frederik Meijer Gardens and Sculpture Park in 1991 (pl. 29) and also at the Marshall Fredericks Sculpture Museum; and *Star Dream Fountain*, 1997 (fig. 347, pl. 31), located in Royal Oak. The latter work, one of his last public works, has arguably the most "public" placement; it is located in a small park just off a busy thoroughfare and near the city's main parking plaza. Its powerful figure grouping, which soars dramatically above visitors, is based on a 1947 preliminary design for the *Cleveland War Memorial Fountain* (fig. 274). Symbolizing mankind's continual quest for spiritual peace, this allegorical work embodies one of the most consistent threads found throughout Fredericks's oeuvre, his hope for a better world.

Fredericks is at his most gentle and whimsical in his sculpture of animals. *The Friendly Dragon* (fig. 331, pl. 30), cast twice in 1991, as a pair for the Meijer Gardens, is a child's magical dream. Like a Maurice Sendak illustration, Frederick's dragon presents a danger that has become approachable, a wild animal that has become as friendly as a pet. The dragon's compact form is globular, his neck rolling alongside and his tail curled up over his back. Its legs are bent so that its belly touches the ground, inviting children to touch and climb upon the amiable beast. The curled-up position emphasizes the dragon's massiveness while bringing it close to human scale. Although long claws and big teeth are still present, their effect is counteracted by a wide and thoroughly disarming smile. The smooth, soft articulation of the body contrasts with the deep, angular carving that articulates the face; both are beautifully crafted. The differences in texture between the folded wings and the body further enliven the surface. While initially the sculpture appears to be a large, solid mass, the rhythmic play of lines between the lumps along the spine, the curved horns, and the wagging tail visually lighten its weight in a playful manner unusual in monumental sculpture.

Most of Frederick's later works are based on small-scale designs from earlier in his career, which were only realized in full-scale late in his life. The mysterious *Sun Worshipper*, originally designed in 1937 (fig. 41), was enlarged and cast to full scale in 1994 (see fig. 336). Fredericks treated this enigmatic, contemporary figure in a classical manner but the result has a spiritual, ritualistic quality. The lower limbs of the female figure, nude from the waist up, are draped with a wide skirt. Her knees are spread wide, with toes and feet together. Her open hands are spread, palms up, and her upturned face is parallel with the sky so that her throat is stretched almost beyond physical capability. The figure's bold form is deeply carved, with angular, archaized features, ranging from the relatively naturalistic hands and feet to the striated, abstracted forms of her hair, which are echoed in the faceted drape of her skirt. The body itself is sensitively rendered with lifelike proportions and curves. Muscular, solid, and androgynous, *Sun Worshipper* is a powerful figure captured in a vulnerable moment. Like the dragon, this figure is curled upon itself and turned psychologically inward, but the dramatic gesture of the upturned face suggests a spiritual quest, a philosophical concept that Fredericks has explored elsewhere.

His last monumental work, *Lord Byron*, designed in 1938 (fig. 53), enlarged by the artist, and cast posthumously in 1998 for the Marshall Fredericks Sculpture Museum (see fig. 356, pl. 32), paradoxically seems to refer back to Fredericks's earliest influences. This literary figure, clearly inspired by Rodin's *Balzac*, strikes a shamelessly dramatic pose: head flung back with his hand on his forehead, heavy cloak partially pulled around his body with the other hand flying out to the side in back. Fredericks, in contrast to the symmetry that generally characterizes his designs, treated each side of the Byron figure in a different manner. Along its right side, the figure is closed and solid. The drop of the heavy cloak does not allow for the articulation of forms or even for any suggestion of the body beneath. Rather, the artist exploits the long, unbroken line of the cloak from the figure's chin to the ground. In contrast, the figure's left side is open and plastic with elbow and knee flung out at an angle from a nipped-in waist. Like *Sun Worshipper*, *Lord Byron* represents an important mid-career design that he was only able to realize in large scale at the end of his career.

The blocky solidity of the right side of *Lord Byron* suggests a reference to *Black Elk*, designed in 1980 (fig. 318), enlarged to full scale by the artist and cast posthumously in 1998 (see fig. 355). Although the cloak completely conceals his body, the strength and dignity of Black Elk is nevertheless conveyed by the figure's mass. This use of the cloak to both conceal and reveal the body in his later sculpture adds a sense of pathos that is missing from Fredericks's early monumental works. The dynamic, unusual treatment of these figures, as well as their uncharacteristic subjects, is tangible evidence that Fredericks continued to push the parameters that had come to define his work.

Curiously, Fredericks never ventured into the ongoing dialogue about pure abstraction that attracted so many sculptors of his generation. While he incorporated abstract elements into his work, he always retained the essence of the figure, and he never strayed far from the narrative, choosing to use his mastery of mass, line, and texture in the service of figurative imagery. His vision, almost entirely consistent throughout his career, found its focal point somewhere between the polemical narratives of mid-twentieth-century American modernism and the resurgence of the figure in European sculpture that he observed after 1950.

The legacy of Marshall Fredericks, in Detroit as well as in the many other cities where his sculpture is installed, updates and personalizes the traditional monument. Fredericks created dynamic, site-specific sculptures that both engage the intellect and tug on the heartstrings, realizing his goals of engaging people with art and humanizing architectural spaces through sculpture. In a time when the efficacy and appropriateness of public sculpture is more than ever in question, his is no small achievement.

MaryAnn Wilkinson

Early Career: 1928–1931

1.

Portrait of an Old Man
1929, black walnut, 23 1/4 inches,
MFSM

2.
Russell Barnett Aitken
1929, terracotta, 17 inches,
MFSM

3.

Chimpanzee and Young
1929, plaster, 12 inches,
location unknown

4.

Wounded Centaur
1929, patinated plaster, 12¹/₄ inches, MFSM

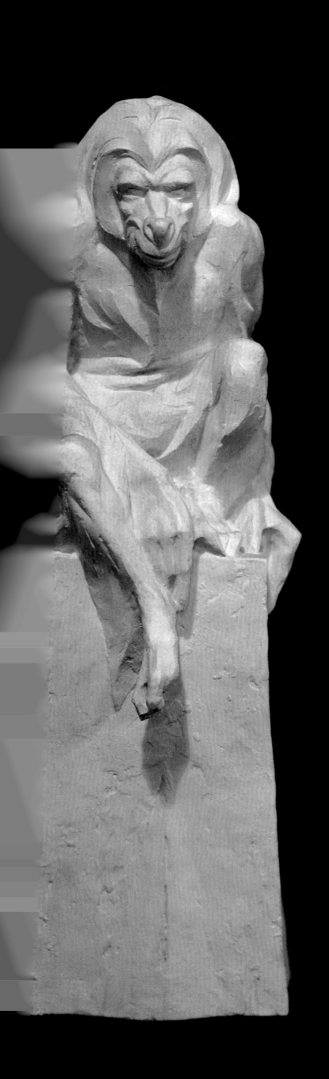

6.
Lute Player
1929, patinated plaster, 11³/₄ inches,
MFSM

5.
Ape Fantasy
1929, plaster, 20 inches,
private collection

Page 19

7.

Playing Bears Fountain
1928–29, stone, 42 inches x 30 feet, completed by
Joseph Motto, Camp Ho-Mita-Koda, Newbury, Ohio

8.

Wood Sprite
1930, black walnut fence rail
on ebony base, 38 inches,
private collection

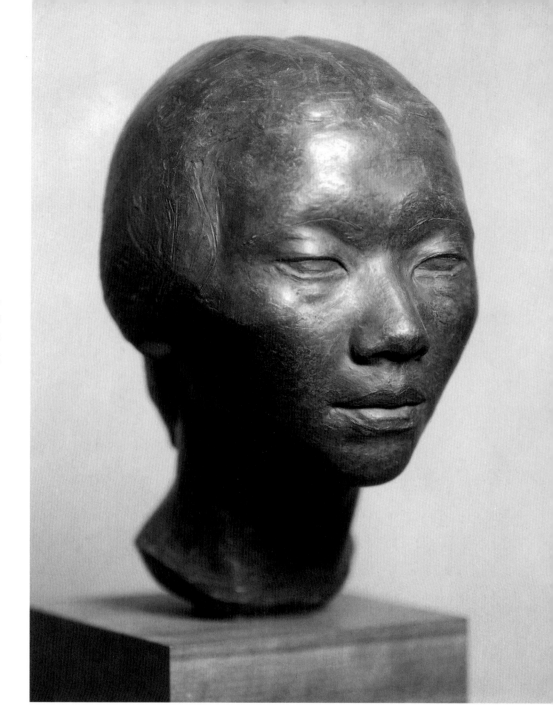

9.
Portrait of a Chinese Actress, (Chinese Girl)
1933, bronze, 12 inches, MFSM

10.
Mary Queen of Scots
1932, bronze, 6 inches, MFSM

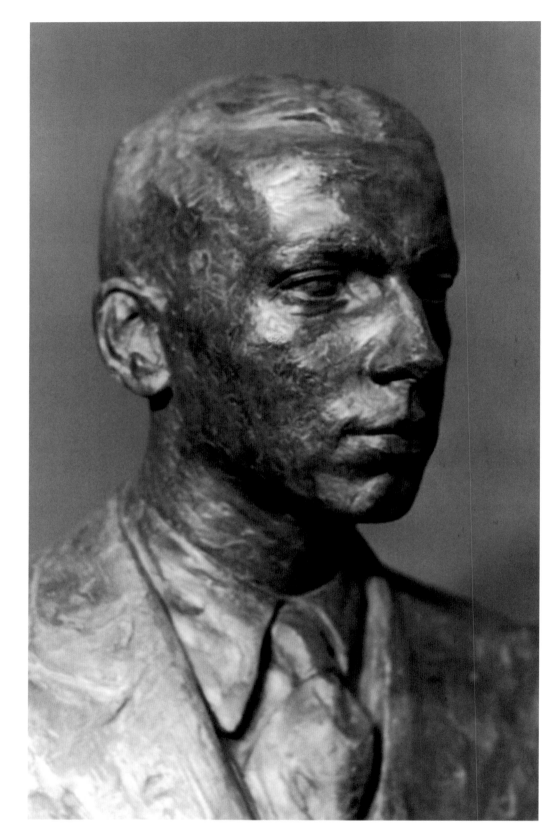

11.
Thomas Morrison Marker
1929, patinated plaster, life-size, location unknown

12.

Portrait of a Young Boy
1931, bronze, 9 inches, private collection

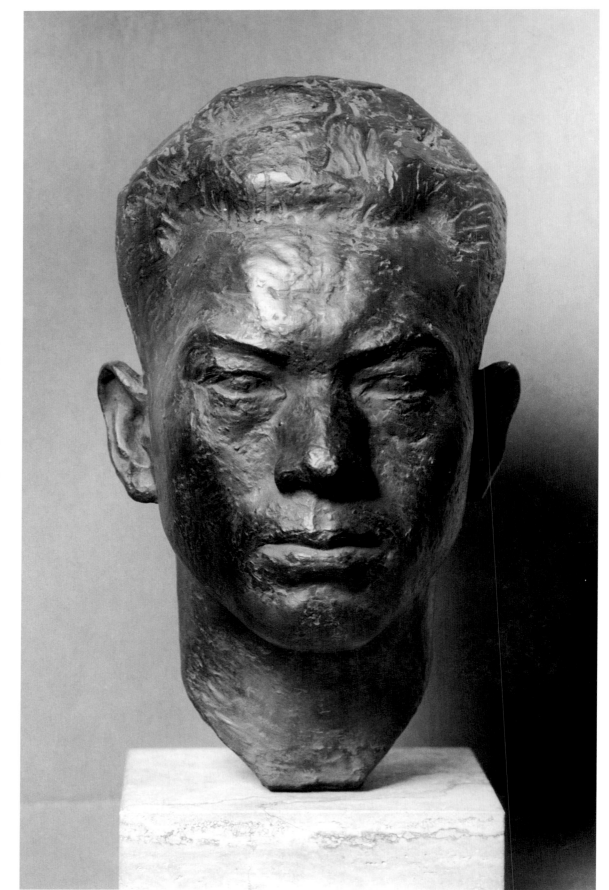

13.
*Nobuji Yoshida
(Portrait of a
Japanese)*
1931, bronze,
15 inches, MFSM

First Prize, Sculpture—
Models or Finished Work,
"Thirteenth Annual
Exhibition," Cleveland
Museum of Art, 1931.

14.
*Portrait of a
German Philosopher*
1931, patinated plaster,
19$\frac{1}{2}$ inches, MFSM

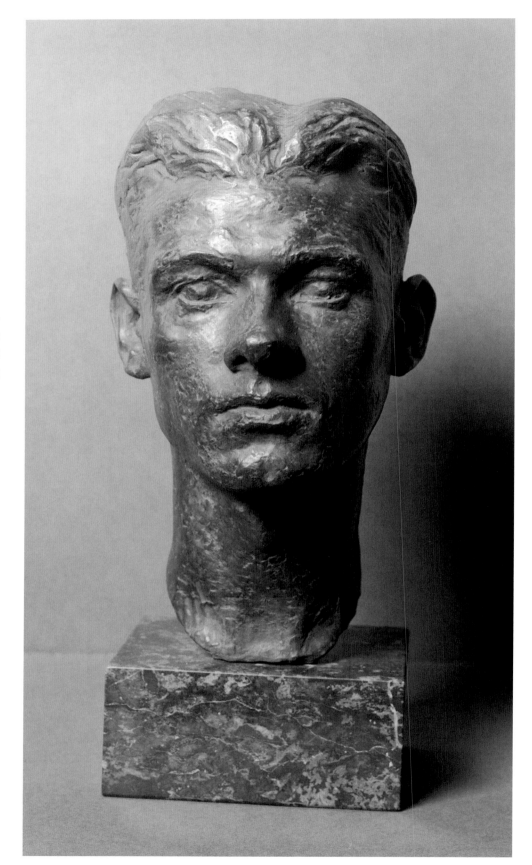

15.

*Portrait of a Young Man
(Lloyd Westbrook)*

1931, bronze, 14 inches, MFSM

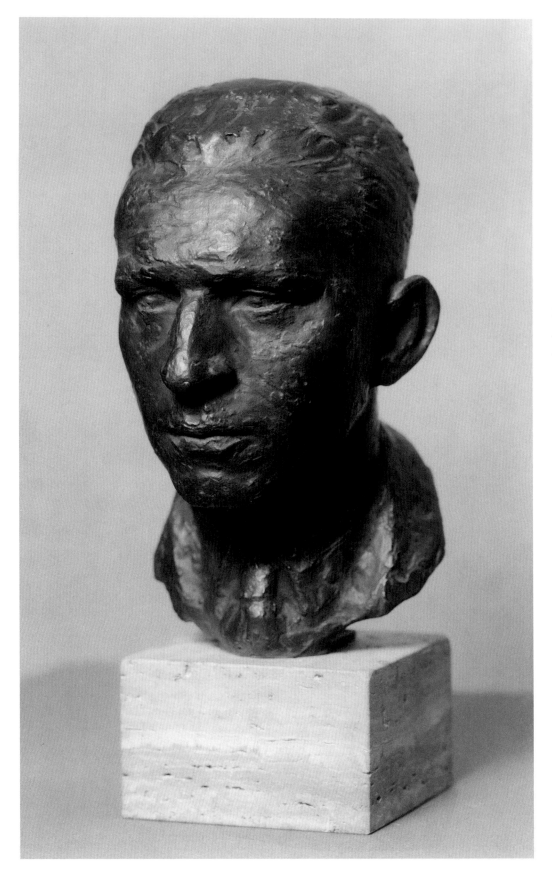

16.
Adelbert Akusy
1931, bronze, 10 inches, MFSM

17.
Mother and Child
1931, porcelain,
10 inches,
destroyed

18.
Polo Player
1931, bronze, 9¹/₂ x 16 inches,
private collection

19.
*Jungle Madonna
and Child*
1931, driftwood on
ebony, 24¹/₂ inches,
MFSM

20.

Siesta (Reclining Lamb)

1930, patinated plaster, 4$^1/_2$ inches, MFSM

21.

Trial Flight (Standing Lamb)

c. 1930, bronze, 7 inches, MFSM

22.

Susanna and the Mirror
1931, porcelain, 6¹/₂ inches, MFSM

23.

Persephone (Bacchante)
1932, small-scale model, bronze,
12½ inches, Cranbrook Art
Museum, Cranbrook Educational
Community, Bloomfield Hills,
Michigan

First Prize, Dance International
1900–1937, "Exhibit of Arts
Relating to the Dance,"
Rockefeller Center, New York.

24.
Portrait of Walker Hickey
1933, plaster, 13 inches, location unknown

25.
Portrait of Marion Kirk
(daughter of Arthur Neville Kirk)
1933, plaster, 12 inches, MFSM

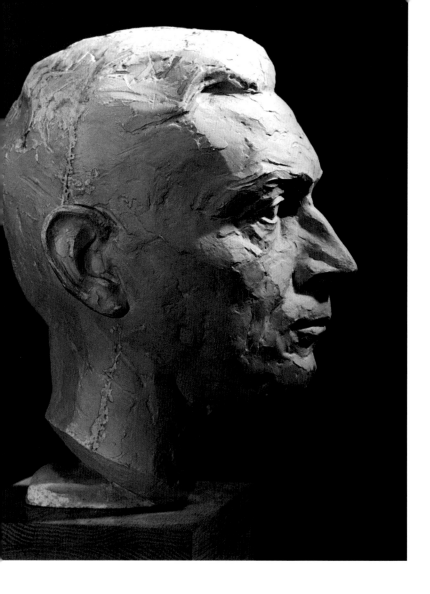

26.
Portrait of Dr. William Oliver Stevens
1935, plaster, 13 ½ inches, MFSM

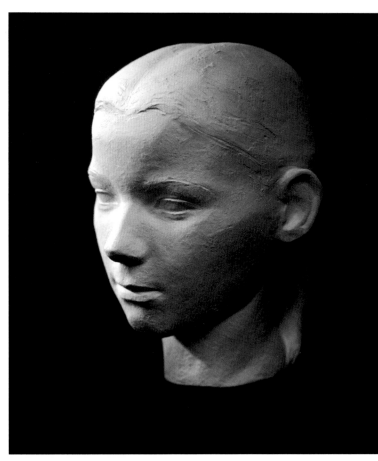

27.
Portrait of Jean Raseman
1933, plaster, 11 inches, MFSM

28.

The Family (Farm Animals)
1941, terracotta, 44 x 38 inches, U.S. Post Office,
Sandwich, Illinois

29.

Horseless Carriage (Model S Ford,
Children and Animals—
Sunday Afternooon)
1939, Plasteline model for limestone relief for
U.S. Post Office, River Rouge, Michigan,
48 x 48 inches, location unknown

30.
O-HI-E-SA (Dr. Charles Eastman)
1935, plaster model for bronze relief commissioned for Boy Scout Camp Ohiyesa (now a YMCA camp), Holly, Michigan, 36 x 48 inches, location unknown

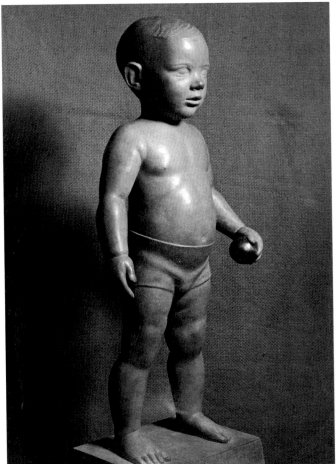

31.
Portrait of Michael Emmet Taylor
1935, bronze, 34$\frac{1}{2}$ inches, private collection

Page 37

32.
Levi L. Barbour Memorial Fountain
1936, bronze and granite, 16 x 20 feet,
Belle Isle, Detroit, Michigan

33.
Leaping Gazelle
(central figure of Levi L. Barbour
Memorial Fountain)
1936, bronze, 16 feet

34.
Rabbit

36.
Hawk

35.
Grouse

37.
Otter

Figures around the base of the Levi L. Barbour Memorial Fountain, 1936, granite, each 30¼ inches

38.
Don Quixote
1937, plaster, 42 inches, MFSM

39.
Sketch model for *Bison*
Plasteline, 8 inches, location unknown

40.
Portrait of Bunichuro Sugimura
1937, plaster, 12 inches, MFSM

41.

Sun Worshipper

1937, bronze, 11 inches, MFSM

42.

Meditation

1937, bronze, 7¹⁄₂ inches, private collection

43.

Clown Musicians
1937, bronze, 27 inches, private collection

44.

Circus Clown
1937, plaster, 27 inches, MFSM

45.

Two Sisters (Mother and Child)
1937, small-scale model of central figures
for proposed fountain, gilt bronze, 19 inches,
Cranbrook Art Museum, Cranbrook
Educational Community, Bloomfield Hills,
Michigan

46.

Two Sisters (Mother and Child)
1937, small-scale plaster model for proposed fountain, 19 inches, MFSM

Figures from *Japanese Goldfish, Lizard, and Frog Fountain*, 1937–38, bronze, Thornlea, Cranbrook Educational Community, Bloomfield Hills, Michigan

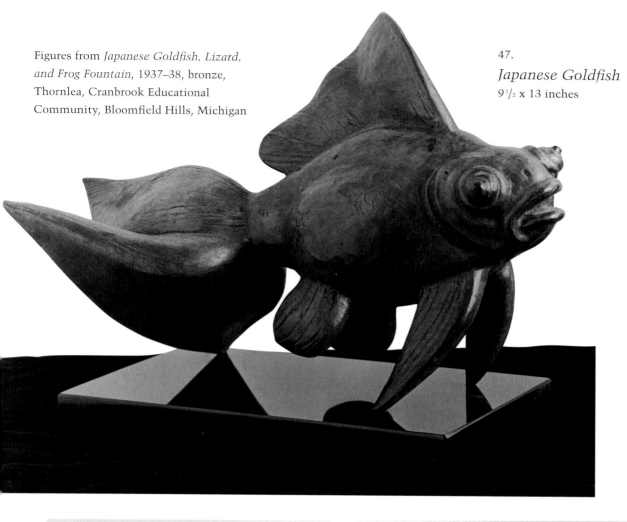

47.

Japanese Goldfish
9 ¹/₂ x 13 inches

48.

Frog (below)
14 inches long

Page 45

49.

Lizard
16 inches long

51.

Portrait of Vincent Anderson
1938, plaster, 13 inches. MFSM

50.

Eve
1937, study for *Two Sisters (Mother and Child)*, gilt bronze,
19 inches, Detroit Institute of Arts

Awarded the David B. Werbe Purchase Prize at the
1946 "Annual Exhibition for Michigan Artists,"
Detroit Institute of Arts.

52.

Torso of a Dancer
1938, black Belgian marble, 40 inches,
Cranbrook Art Museum,
Cranbrook Educational Community,
Bloomfield Hills, Michigan

Bronze version awarded the
Anna Scripps Whitcomb Prize at the
1938 "Annual Exhibition for Michigan
Artists," Detroit Institute of Arts.

53.

Lord Byron

1938, plaster, 32 inches, MFSM

54.

Pioneer Woman and Ox
1938, patinated plaster, 16³/₄ inches, MFSM

55.

Indian and Buffalo
1938, patinated plaster, 16¹/₂ inches, MFSM

56.

The Thinker

1938, black Mellen granite, 26 inches (base: 48 inches),
Cranbrook Art Museum, Cranbrook Educational
Community, Bloomfield Hills, Michigan

View of location on front steps of the museum,
adjacent to main entrance.

57.
The Thinker (details)

58.

Page 51

59.

Lovesick Clown (Pagliacci)
bronze with gold-plated arrow, 29 inches

60.

Juggler, Acrobat, and Lovesick Clown
1938, bronze, private collection

62.
Juggler
bronze, 29³/₄ inches

61.
Acrobat
bronze, 39³/₄ inches   Page 53

63.
Sketch model for 1938 Radio City Music Hall Competition
New York City, patinated plaster, 36 x 28 inches, MFSM

64.

Sketch model (female)
for *Celestial Fountain*
1938, proposal for 1939 New York
World's Fair, plaster, 15 inches, MFSM

65.

Sketch model (male) for *Celestial Fountain*
1938, proposal for 1939 New York World's Fair, plaster,
18¹/₂ inches, MFSM

66.

Achievement
1938, bronze, 37 inches, location unknown
Originally owned by People's Outfitting Company, Detroit

67.

Animal Kingdoms—Reptile

1939, bronze, 9¹/₂ inches, private collection

68.
Animal Kingdoms—Fish
1939, bronze, 9 ¹/₂ inches, location unknown

69.
Animal Kingdoms—Mammal
1939, bronze, 9 inches, private collection

70.

Animal Kingdoms—Bird

1939, bronze, 9 inches, location unknown

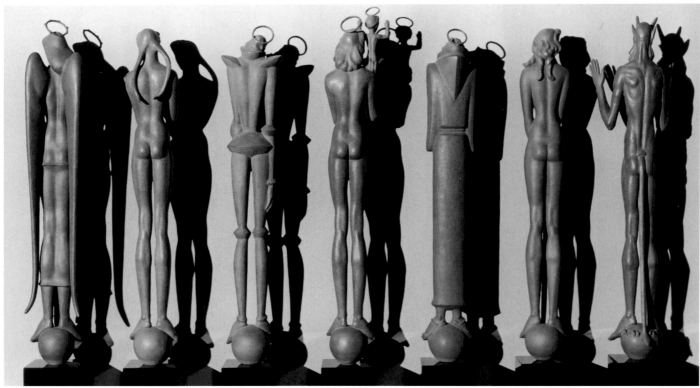

71.
Saints and Sinners
1939, 34 ¹/₂ inches, bronze, private collection

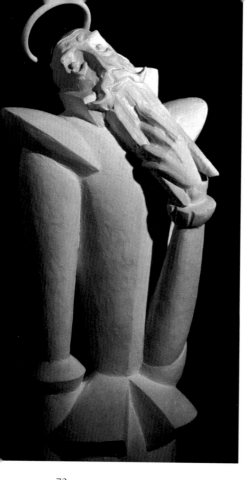

72.

Warrior Saint
plaster, 32 inches, MFSM

Details from *Saints and Sinners*

74.

Holy Mother and Child
plaster, 34 1/2 inches, MFSM

73.

*Sinner with Serpent
(Temptation)*
plaster, 32 inches, MFSM

75.

Baboon Playing a Mandolin
1939, bronze, 14 inches, private collection

76.

Baboon and Baby Chimpanzee
1939, bronze, 14¹/₂ inches, private collection

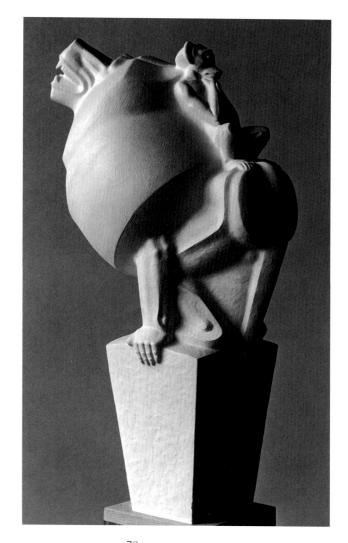

77.

Baboon and Sitting Friend
1939, plaster, 31½ inches, private collection

78.

Baboon and Sleeping Child
1939, plaster, 27¾ inches,
private collection

79.

*Baboon of the Theatre
Playing a Ham*
1938, patinated plaster, 14 inches, MFSM

Designed as a bronze trophy for St.
Dunstan's Theatre Guild, Cranbrook
Educational Community, Bloomfield
Hills, Michigan.

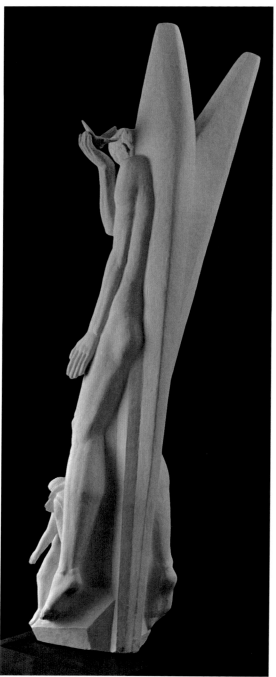

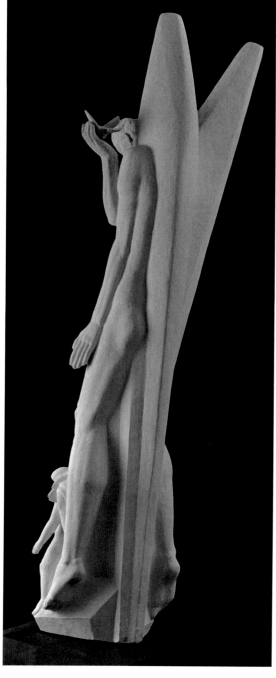

80.

Guardian Angel

1939, plaster, 37¹/₂ inches

Sketch models for 1939 New York World's Fair
United States Building Competition

81.

Pro Patria

1939, plaster, 38 inches

82.

Baboon Fountain
(Board of Directors Fountain)
1939, cast stone in glass basin, 14 feet, including bases

Created for the Glass Industries Building at the 1939
New York World's Fair, Flushing Meadow, New York,
subsequently destroyed.

83.

Baby Baboon
(centerpiece of Baboon Fountain)
1939, cast stone, 44 inches, including base

84.

Baboon and Baby Baboon
(from Baboon Fountain)
Glass Industries Building,
1939 New York World's Fair

85.
Baboon (one of five adult baboons
from Baboon Fountain)
cast stone, 14 feet, including base

86.
Baboon (one of five adult baboons
from Baboon Fountain)
cast stone, 14 feet, including base

87.

Horace H. Rackham Educational Memorial Building, Detroit

Harley, Ellington and Day, architects

Views of the front façade and entrance.

88–89.
Education Sciences (above)
Steel Workers (below)
1939, marble, 15 feet and 9 feet
Details from Rackham Building

90.
Chinese Astronomer
1939, marble, 8 feet

91.
Education
1939, marble, 4 feet

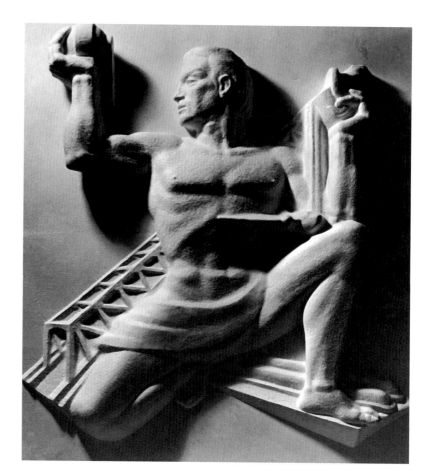

92.
Electrical, Steel, Civil, and
Railroad Engineering
1939, marble, 8 feet

93.

Knowledge
1939, marble, 4 feet

Details from Rackham Building, Detroit

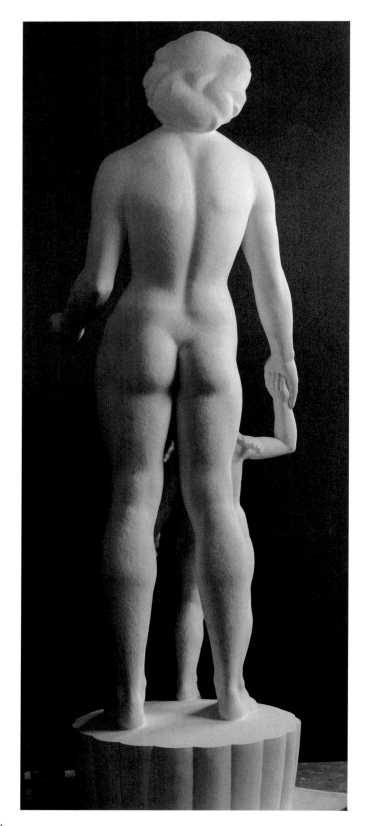

94.

Two Sisters (Mother and Child)

1942, full-scale plaster model for central figures in Kingswood School fountain (see fig. 300),
5 feet, MFSM

95–96.

Two Sisters (Mother and Child)

(details)

97.

Moray Eel and Fish

1941, green granite, 15 x 27 ½ x 21 inches, Cranbrook Art Museum, Cranbrook Educational
Community, Bloomfield Hills, Michigan

Honorable Mention in Sculpture, "Fifty-Second Annual Exhibition of American Paintings
and Sculpture," Art Institute of Chicago, 1941.

98.

Siberian Ram

1941, plaster, 22 inches, MFSM

Drawings: 1930–1960

The Garden in Lidingö

Oh, God above,
I silently stand,
Before this Masterpiece
From Thine own hand,
Created by Thee,
From Infinite Mind,
And given to bless,
Thine own Mankind.

Oh, God I pray,
That I should be,
That Blessed One,
With gift from Thee,
To bring to Man,
Such Holy Thought,
As these chosen few,
Alone have brought.

One single thing,
Is that, I ask,
One single thing,
Which ere shall last,
Until the End of Time and Man,
Oh God I pray,
Choose me to be,
The one to bring
A thought from Thee.

—MMF, written at Millesgården, 1930

99.

Self-Portrait

1930, photo-lithograph on paper, 11 x 8¹/₂ inches,
private collection

100.

Portrait of a Black Woman
c. 1930, charcoal and chalk on paper,
25 x 19 inches, private collection

101.

Portrait of an Older Man
c. 1930, charcoal and chalk on paper,
25 x 19 inches, MFSM

102.

Morocco
1931, pencil, ink, and conté crayon on paper,
8⁷/₈ x 9³/₄ inches, MFSM

103.

India (portrait of mother and child)
1945, watercolor and ink on paper, 4¹/₄ x 3¹/₄
inches, private collection

104.
Life drawing of female nude kneeling
c. 1950s, pencil, charcoal or conté crayon, and chalk
on paper, 19 1/2 x 15 inches, MFSM

105.
Life drawing of female nude reclining
c. 1950s, conté crayon on paper, 14 x 22 inches, MFSM

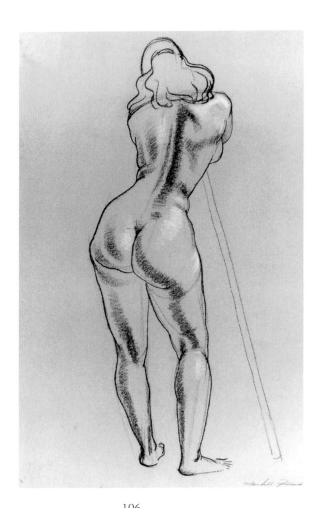

106.

Life drawing of female nude standing
c. 1950s, charcoal and chalk on paper,
19 x 12 1/2 inches, private collection

107.
Life drawing of male nude
c. 1950s, charcoal on paper, 18 x 13 inches,
private collection

108.
Male torso and face
c. 1950s, pencil and gouache
on paper, 17⁷/₈ x 11⁷/₈,
private collection

109.
Sketches from life (deer head studies)
c. 1950s, pencil on paper, 11⁷/₈ x 17³/₄ inches, MFSM

110.

*The Consciousness of Mankind Rising Above the Earth
into the Expanding Universe*

n.d., pencil and watercolor on board, 20 x 38 inches, private collection
Inscribed at lower left, "with fountain in gold and silver-colored metals"

111.

Project drawing of planetary sphere for science library

n.d., pencil, colored pencil, and watercolor on board, 12³/₈ x 18³/₈ inches,

private collection

112.

Stag hood ornament

c. 1950s, pencil, gouache, and pastel on board,
20 x 28 inches, private collection

Project drawing for *Fabulous Fish Fountain*

1966, pencil, watercolor, and gouache on board, 25 x 38¹/₂ inches,
private collection

114.

Corregidor Bataan Memorial

c. 1950, location unknown

Drawing for a proposed memorial in honor of the soldiers who lost their
lives in the Bataan Death March, April 1942.

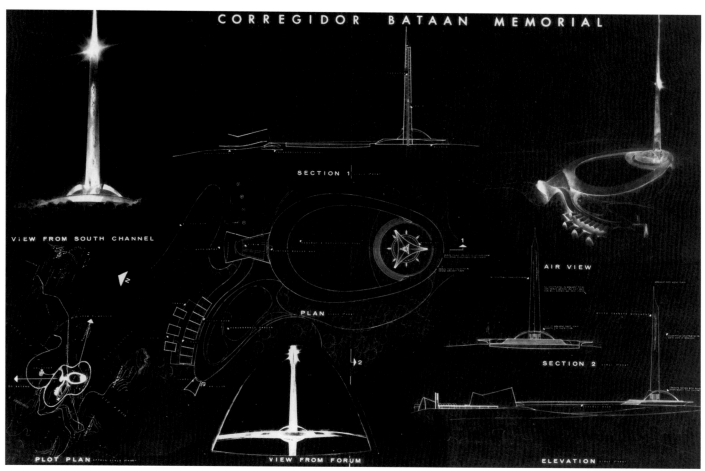

Post-War Career: 1946–1998

115.
Fredericks working on
Plasteline model of
the *Spirit of Kentucky*

We are all aware of the countless instances where the emotional and spiritual beauty of sculpture has fused with the functional and practical forms of architecture, and the two working together have achieved a result far more beautiful than either could have achieved alone. This to me is the ideal—the various arts with a common purpose, mutually helpful, one complementing and assisting the other, all working harmoniously toward the accomplishment of a beautiful and functional objective.

Just as in alliance with architecture, sculpture gains in purpose, importance, usefulness, scale and greater appreciation, so architecture in alliance with sculpture can gain in added beauty, richness, character, interest, warmth, and in those spiritual and personal qualities which give a structure meaning to the people who use and see it. Sculpture can be used to identify a building with its purpose, to indicate the spirit in which the building was conceived, to give that building something completely personal, which no other building has, and to unify the different elements in a building or group of buildings.

Somehow architecture, the bonding agent, must embrace the other arts, and all must fuse into a beautiful, functional, and harmonious whole. This can be accomplished only by the consistent and complete and intelligent collaboration of all, working harmoniously toward the accomplishment of a beautiful objective—an environment of beauty as a part of everyday living.

— MMF, excerpt from "Architecture and Sculpture," Journal of the American Institute of Architects, July 1952.

116.

Spirit of Kentucky

1948, bronze on polished black granite, 16 feet,

Courier-Journal Building, Louisville, Kentucky,

Joseph H. Kolbrook, architect

117.
Project drawing for *Spirit of Kentucky*, 1946, pencil on paper,
5¹/₂ x 6¹/₂ inches, private collection

Models for *Spirit of Kentucky*,
Courier-Journal Building, Louisville

118.
*Pioneer Family and
Animals of the Region*
1948, small-scale model, plaster,
22 x 36 inches, MFSM

119.
*Riverboats and
Giant Catfish*
1948, plaster, 46 x 62 inches,
MFSM

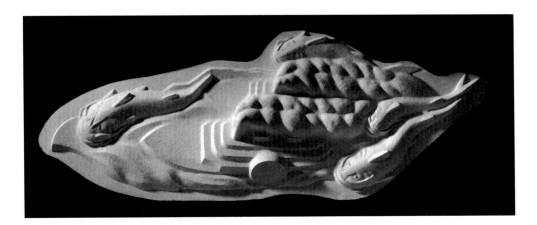

120.
*Huckleberry Finn and
Tom Sawyer Observing
the Riverboats and
Giant Catfish*
1948, small-scale model, plaster,
17 x 17 inches, MFSM

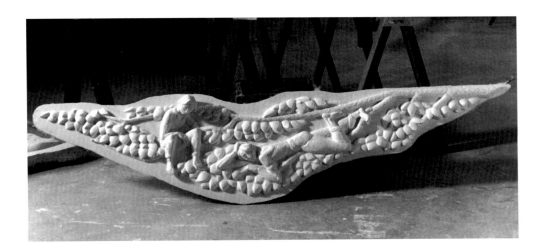

121.
Raccoons
1948, plaster,
18 x 27¹/₂ inches, MFSM

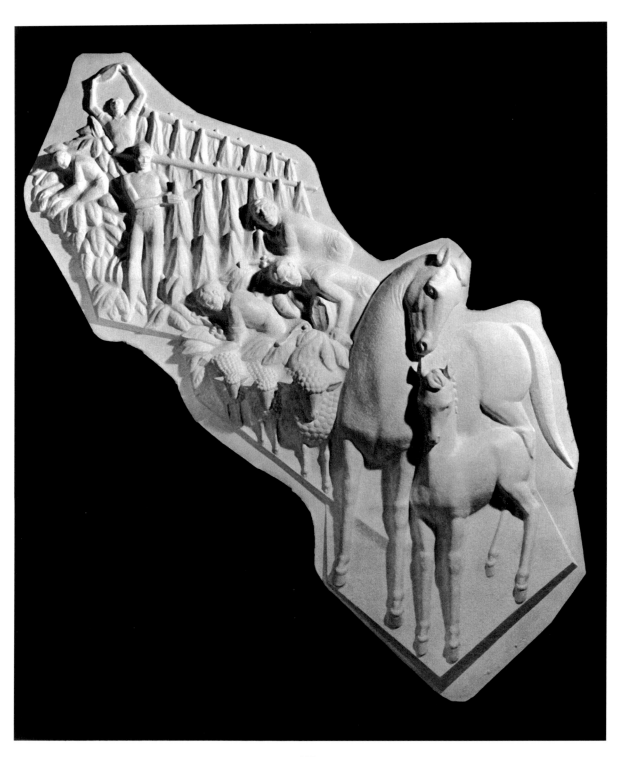

122.

Thoroughbreds, Sheep and
Tobacco Farmers
1948, plaster, location unknown

Model for *Spirit of Kentucky*, Courier-Journal Building, Louisville

123.
Eaton War Memorial Eagle
1948, bronze on marble,
38 x 42 inches, Eaton Manufacturing
Corporation, Cleveland, Ohio

124.
Young Knight
1949, German silver, 30 x 16 ½ inches,
Ottawa High School, Grand Rapids,
Michigan

125.

Administration Building
(now the Literature, Science and Arts Building),
University of Michigan, Ann Arbor,
Harley, Ellington and Day, architects.

Thirty cast aluminum, seven limestone, and two bronze reliefs
decorate the façades of the building.

126.
Dream of the Young Man
1949, Plasteline, 5 feet long

127.
Dream of the Young Girl
(left) and *Dream of the*
Young Man (right)
1949, bronze, 12 feet and 5 feet long
Main (east) entrance.

128.
Naturalist (below) and
Adventurer (above)
1949, limestone, 36 inches long
Side entrance with west entrance
(showing *Hiawatha* and *Aesop*,
8 feet) in background.

129.
Naturalist
1949, plaster model for one of
seven limestone reliefs, 36 inches
long, location unknown

130–132.
Man and the Universe (left)
Hands of God (right)
Student Motif (below)
1949, small-scale plaster models for
aluminum reliefs, 14–16 inches,
MFSM

Models for the Administration
Building (now the Literature,
Science and Arts Building),
University of Michigan, Ann Arbor

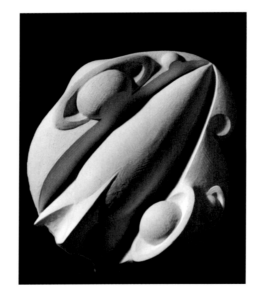

133.

Project drawing
for *Scientists*
c. 1948, pencil, watercolor, and
ink on paper, 5 x 7 ¼ inches,
private collection

134.

Scientists
1949, plaster model for one of seven limestone
reliefs, 36 inches long, location unknown

135.

Victory Eagle **and three of seven carved pylons**
1950, marble, Veterans Memorial Building (now the UAW-Ford Program Center), Detroit, Harley Ellington and Day, architects

This work won a Fine Arts Medal from the American Institute of Architects in 1952.

The problem was to take a natural object, one especially familiar to everyone, and simplify it in form to something almost architectural in quality, absolutely abstract in form and line, to tie in with the masses and character of the building, yet retain the character and meaning of the natural object. Also, it was necessary to indicate power and motion of the eagle, still make it an integral part of the marble wall, solid yet mobile, an architectural entity and yet imbue it with the spirit of life. — MMF, from "Import of Sculptural Work," *Michigan Architect and Engineer*, April 1950.

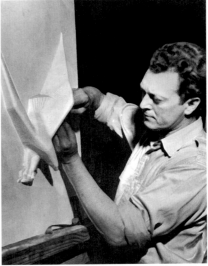

136.
Fredericks carving small-scale plaster model of *Victory Eagle*, 1947

137.

Aerial view, *Victory Eagle* and pylons, 1950

Much of the design for the current layout of
Hart Plaza and the surrounding area, including the Veterans Memorial, Ford Auditorium,
the City-County Building, and Cobo Hall,
was originally conceived by Eliel and Eero
Saarinen in their 1947 civic plan.

138.

Marble sections of 30-foot *Victory Eagle*, carved
at Vermont Marble Company, Proctor, Vermont,
prior to installation in Detroit

Page 94

139.

"In the hearts of all mankind is the Eternal Hope for a Universal Peace."—inscribed on the Peace Pylon. View of carved pylons from the former Veterans Memorial Building. The pylons commemorate important military events in the city's history from the *Founding of Detroit* to the *Peace Pylon*, in honor of World War II. Shown at far right is the pylon representing World War I.

140–144.

Left to right:

Founding of Detroit
French explorer Cadillac and Father Gabriel Richard

Indian Wars
Treaty with Chief Pontiac

Battle of the Great Lakes
War of 1812, General Perry's victory

Civil War
Abraham Lincoln, Generals Lee and Grant

Spanish-American War
Surrender of Spanish troops to Roosevelt's
Rough Riders

1950, Plasteline models for carved marble pylons,
20 feet

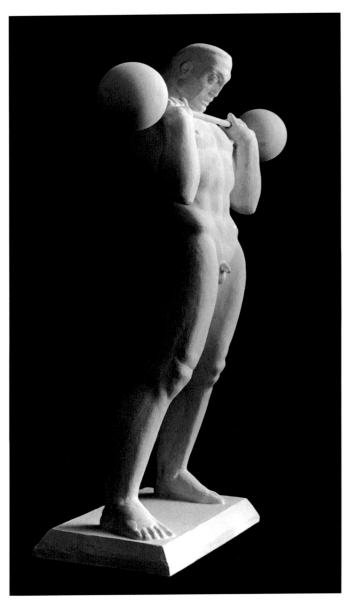

145.

Strong Man
1950, plaster, 17 inches, MFSM

146.

Henry and Edsel Ford
c. 1950, preliminary plaster model for *Henry Ford Memorial*,
18 ¹/₄ inches, MFSM

This particular version was never realized; the *Henry Ford Memorial* was not completed until twenty years later.

147.
Fredericks and his assistant Thomas Marker in the Royal Oak studio, enlarging the *American Eagle* from small-scale plaster model to full-scale Plasteline model

148.

American Eagle
(Ann Arbor War Memorial Eagle)
1950, front view, bronze on granite, 12 feet,
University of Michigan Stadium, Ann Arbor

"In Honor of the Men and Women of the
University of Michigan Who Gave Their Lives
to Their Country, 1946"

Alternate view

149.

Childhood Friends

1950, bronze, 6 feet, Jefferson Memorial Elementary
School, Wyandotte, Michigan

150.

George Gough Booth and Ellen Scripps Booth Memorial

1950, gilt bronze on limestone, diameter 21 inches, Cranbrook Institute of
Science, Cranbrook Educational Community, Bloomfield Hills, Michigan

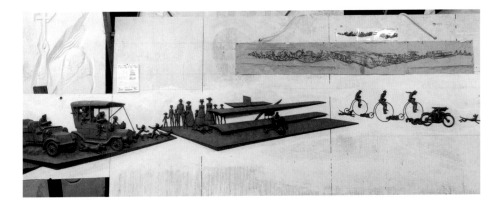

151.
Working drawing and a section
of the Plasteline model for the
reliefs designed for Union Station,
Fort Street, Detroit, 1951

152.

The Romance of Transportation
1951, polished aluminum, 44 feet long

Originally installed at Union Station, Fort Street, Detroit, the reliefs were relocated
to the B&O Railroad Museum, Baltimore, Maryland, following demolition of the depot.

153.

"Trains and Automobiles"
(detail of right side)

154.

"The Opening of the West"
(detail of left side)

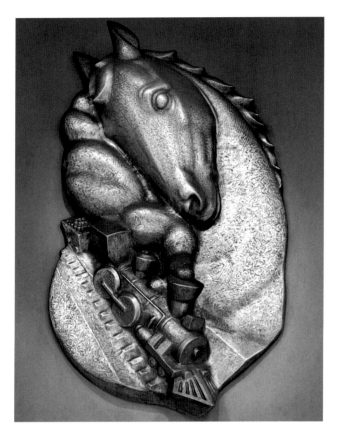

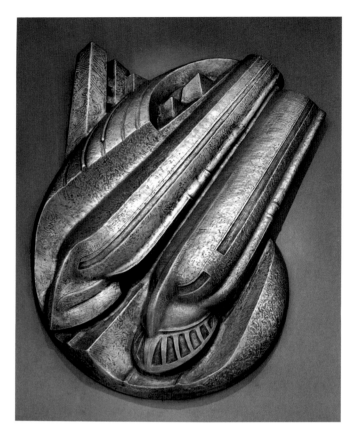

155.

Horse and Antique Trains

1951, polished aluminum, 39 x 20 inches

156.

Modern Trains

1951, polished aluminum, 34$^1/_2$ x 23 inches

Motifs from *The Romance of Transportation*, Union Station, Fort Street, Detroit

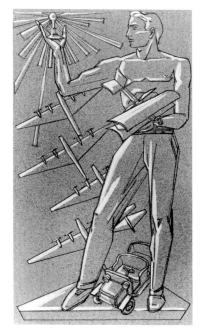

157.

Johnny Appleseed

Ohio's legendary hero teaching a family to plant a tree

158.

Pioneers and Early Settlers

Representing the romance and hardships of westward expansion into Ohio

159.

Aeronautical Pioneering

Showing one of the Wright brothers with the first motor-driven airplane. The final relief was revised to include other Ohio industries, ceramics and agriculture (see fig. 165).

Project drawings for the Ohio Union reliefs, 1951, conté crayon and gouache on board, image size 13 x 7³/₈ inches, private collection

160.

Fredericks working on full-scale Plasteline model of *Ceramics, Agriculture, and Aeronautical Pioneering*, one of six limestone reliefs for the Ohio Union Building, Ohio State University, Columbus

Working drawing appears at left.

161.

*The Steel Industry and
River Freighters*

162.

Education and Government

163.

Johnny Appleseed

1951, Plasteline models for three of six
limestone reliefs, 8 feet

164.

Pioneers and Early Settlers

165.

*Ceramics, Agriculture, and
Aeronautical Pioneering*

166.

*Indians of the
Ohio River Valley*

1951, three of six limestone reliefs, 8 feet

167.

Fredericks carving *Johnny Appleseed*
relief in situ, c. 1950, Ohio Union
Building, Ohio State University,
Columbus

168.
Working from plaster model,
Fredericks carving *Ceramics,
Agriculture, and Aeronautical
Pioneering* relief in situ, c. 1950,
Ohio Union Building

169.
Ohio Union Building, Ohio State University, Columbus, Ohio,
Bellman, Gillett and Richards, architects

The Ohio Union reliefs won an Honorable Mention in Sculpture
from the Architectural League of New York in 1955.

170.

Mary A. Rackham

1951, bronze on marble, 38 inches, Horace H. Rackham
Memorial Educational Building, Detroit

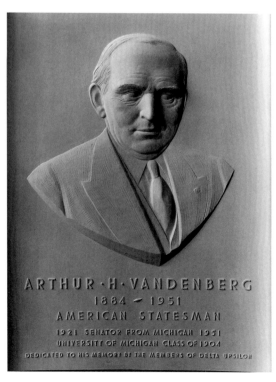

171.

Arthur H. Vandenberg

1951, bronze, 30 x 35 inches, Rackham Memorial
Building, University of Michigan, Ann Arbor

172.
Fredericks working on Plasteline model of *The Steel Industry*, one of sixteen fiberglass polyester resin laminate reliefs for the Ford Rotunda, Dearborn, Michigan

173.
Machine Tool and Die Industry

174.
Crating and Shipping

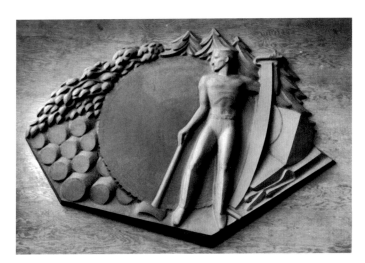

175.
The Lumber Industry

176.
The Petroleum Industry

177.
The Rubber Industry

178–180.
Ford Rotunda, Dearborn, Michigan
Albert Kahn, architect, dome by Buckminster Fuller
(building destroyed by fire in 1962)
1953, fiberglass polyester resin laminate reliefs depicting
industries related to the manufacture of automobiles

The sixteen reliefs won the Gold Medal in Sculpture from
the Architectural League of New York in 1956.

Opposite page:
1953, Plasteline models for fiberglass
polyester resin laminate reliefs, 8 feet

181.

The Boy and Bear

1954, small-scale plaster model,
11³/₄ inches, MFSM

182.
Stone carvers using plaster model as
guide for carving out the rough form
of the bear from limestone

183.
Plasteline model for limestone carving,
8¹/₂ feet

184.

The Boy and Bear

1954, limestone and gilt bronze, 8^1/$_2$ feet,
Northland Center, Southfield, Michigan,
Victor Gruen, architect

185.

*Mankind and Primates
(The Family of Man)*

1955, aluminum, 21 inches x 9½ feet,

Holden Amphitheater and Great Ape House,

Detroit Zoological Institute, Royal Oak,

Michigan, W. Roy Akitt, architect (building

replaced by new primate center in the 1980s)

186–187.
Furniture and toys for the great apes at the Detroit Zoological Institute

1955, stainless steel and reinforced fiberglass

From left to right: monkey-go-round, double trapeze ring, trapeze pallet, climbing tree

From left to right: mushroom seat and weighing scales, pallet stools, sleeping pallet, spring exercising ladder

Fredericks studied the orangutans, gibbons and chimpanzees at the zoo for months to determine their needs, selecting fiberglass and stainless steel for hygienic reasons and bright colors that the apes seemed to like.

188.
Cotton Pickers

189.
Steers

190.
Gold Miner

Plasteline models for three of a series of twelve designs representing national products that were created for a 1939 national competition, each 10½ x 8 inches

These three reliefs and the two pictured at left were later put together as a group by the artist.

191.
Sheep
(The Guests Have Arrived)
Plaster model for 1955 bronze version, 10½ x 8 inches, MFSM

192.
Chimpanzee (Philosopher)
1955, bronze, 10½ x 8 inches, private collection

193.

Indian and Bears

20¹⁄₂ x 10¹⁄₂ inches

194.

*Indian, Deer,
and Wolves*

20¹⁄₄ x 11 inches

195.

Pony Express Rider

20¹⁄₄ x 9¹⁄₂ inches

196.

Indian Rider

20¹⁄₄ inches x 9¹⁄₂ inches

Series of four Plasteline
models, c. 1940, later cast
as bronze reliefs, c. 1955

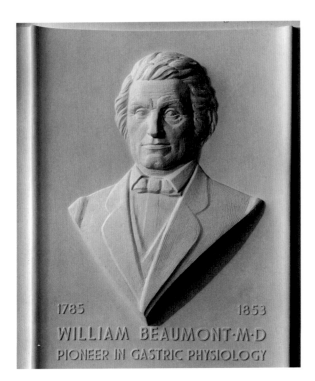

197.

William Beaumont, M.D.

1955, plaster, 35 x 30 inches, MFSM

Copper-patinated bronze versions of this work are
in the collections of the Mackinac Island Museum,
Mackinac Island, Michigan, and William Beaumont
Hospital, Royal Oak, Michigan.

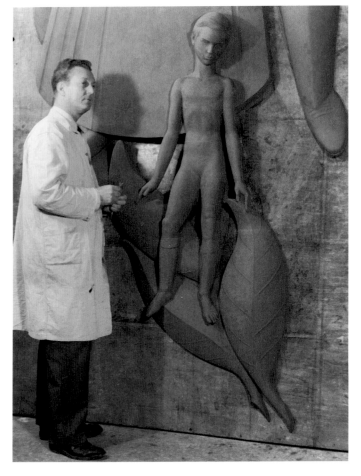

198.

Fredericks working on Plasteline model of
The Family Protected by Healing Herbs, 1955

"The leaves of the tree were for the healing of
the nation" Revelation 22:2

199.

The Family Protected by Healing Herbs
1955, aluminum, 16 feet, William Beaumont Hospital,
Royal Oak, Michigan, Ellerbe and Company, architects

Awarded the Gold Medal in Sculpture by the
Architectural League of New York in 1956.

200.

Justice and Knowledge Imparted to Youth

1955, Plasteline, 4 feet

201.

Wisdom Joining with Friendship and Understanding

1955, plaster, 4 feet

202.

Justice Is Served While Employing Compassion and Kindness

1955, plaster, 4 feet

203.

Justice Encompasses Knowledge and Technology

1955, plaster, 4 feet

204.

A Father and Mother Teaching a Lesson in Charity
1955, bronze on marble, 4 feet

Family and Justice Reliefs, five scenes in fourteen courtrooms, City-County Building (now the Coleman A. Young Municipal Center), Detroit

205.

Seal of Wayne County
1955, bronze, 32 inches, City-County Building, Detroit
A marble carving of this seal, 10 feet in diameter, along with a marble rendition of the *Seal of the City of Detroit*, is located on the wall behind *The Spirit of Detroit* at the main entrance to the building (see fig. 230).

206.

Flying Wild Geese

1955, small-scale model, bronze, 14 1/4 inches,
MFSM

207.

Flying Wild Geese

1955, bronze on Norwegian emerald-pearl granite, 40 inches
(10 feet including base), Alvin Macauley Memorial, Elmwood
Cemetery, Detroit

208

Five Nordic Swans Fountain
1956–60, plaster, wood, and metal site model,
8 x 42 x 40 inches, MFSM

Architectural drawings for the Henry and
Edsel Ford Auditorium include a proposal,
c. 1956, for a Tracy W. McGregor Memorial
Fountain that incorporates this design; a
revised version was proposed for Shain Park
in Birmingham, Michigan, c. 1960. Neither
project was ever realized.

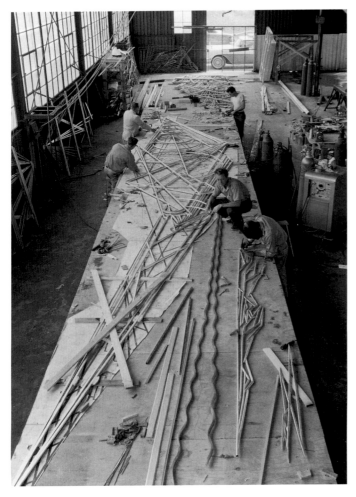

209.
Fredericks and assistants piecing together metal sections for
The Ford Empire in a warehouse rented as a temporary studio
to accommodate the 145-foot span of the sculpture, Clarkston,
Michigan, c. 1955–56

210.
*Harlequins (Juggler, Acrobat, and
Lovesick Clown)* and *Circus Parade*
West wall grouping, 14 feet

211.
Harlequin with Concertina
c. 1955–56, study for relief at Henry and
Edsel Ford Auditorium, conté crayon on
board, 19 x 14 inches, private collection

212.

The Ford Empire on foyer wall with *Harlequins*, *Ballerina*, and *Orchestral Parade* in the wings, Henry and Edsel Ford Auditorium, Detroit, O'Dell, Hewlett and Luchenbach, architects

The people of the earth are divided up into different nations, different religions, different political philosophies, different languages and customs. But there are no barriers in the appreciation of fine artistic endeavor. This is an area where man can communicate with man in any part of the world. Art is a universal language. Art speaks directly to some inner sense of harmony. It touches people's hearts and minds, lifts them out of their daily lives, gives them joy, and even at times a kind of ecstasy . . . A European can feel awe and reverence toward a Chinese porcelain. A Japanese symphony conductor can perform Beethoven superbly. An American can be deeply moved by an African woodcarving. Our political philosophy is different from that of Communist Russia, and yet when we see a performance of the Bolshoi ballet, all differences become non-existent, in admiration and enjoyment of the art.
—MMF, from "Thoughts About the Universality of Art," an undated manuscript, MFSM archives.

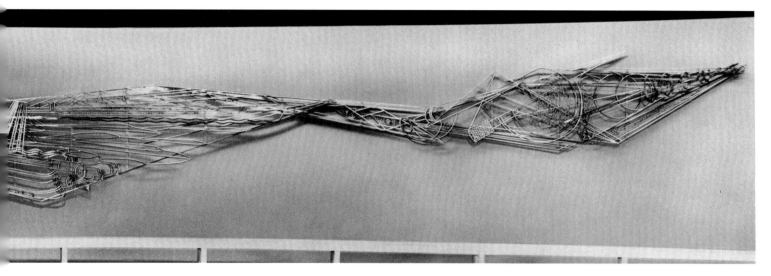

213.

The Ford Empire
1956, repoussé and formed metals: copper, nickel, brass, stainless steel, and aluminum, plated with gold, zinc, and cadmium, 145 feet long, Henry and Edsel Ford Auditorium, Detroit

"The Creation of the Universe" and "Forces and Products of Nature" (left) together with "The Skills and Intelligence of Man" (right) coalesce in the center of the sculpture with the Ford Rotunda, Ford Headquarters, factories, and aircraft and car development representing the Ford empire.

214.
Fredericks working on Plasteline
model of hands for *Youth in the
Hands of God*, 1956

215.
*Youth in the Hands
of God*
View from below.

216.

Youth in the Hands of God
1956, aluminum, 20 feet, created for the New Dallas Public Library, Dallas, Texas,
George L. Dahl, architect (relocated to MFSM)

217.
Reclining Lion
1957, project drawing for The Lion
and Mouse, pencil on board, 18 x
27¹/₂ inches, private collection

Includes a description at lower
left, "Limestone-with gold claws
and mouse"

218.
Lion and Monkey
1957, sketch model, bronze,
8 x 12 inches, MFSM

219.
Mouse of *The Lion and Mouse*
1957, bronze, 5¹/₂ inches with base,
MFSM

220.
The Lion and Mouse
1957, full-scale Plasteline model for limestone carving,
5 x 9 feet

221.
The Lion and Mouse
1957, small-scale bronze model for limestone carving,
13 ½ x 24 inches, private collection

222.
The Lion and Mouse
1957, limestone and gilt bronze, 5 x 9 feet, Eastland Center,
Harper Woods, Michigan, Victor Gruen, architect

223.

Anniversary Baboons
1957, bronze, 12 inches, Alden B. Dow
Home and Studio, Midland, Michigan

224.

The Spirit of Detroit
1958, sketch model, bronze and
gilt bronze, 11 inches, MFSM

225.

The Spirit of Detroit
1958, small-scale refined model,
bronze and gilt bronze, 10¹/₂ inches
(presentation box: 14¹/₂ x 18 x 7¹/₂ inches)

Presented to former President Dwight D.
Eisenhower during his visit to Detroit for
the National Auto Show, October 17, 1963.

226.

The Spirit of Detroit
1958, small-scale refined model,
bronze and gilt bronze, 10¹/₂ inches,
MFSM

Models for work commissioned for the
City-County Building (now the Coleman A.
Young Municipal Center), Detroit

227.

The Spirit of Detroit
1958, quarter-scale model, Plasteline, 6 feet

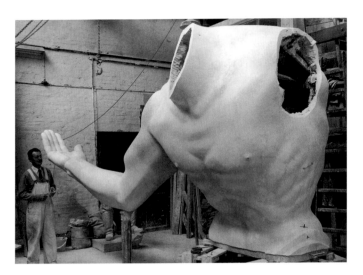

228.
Fredericks working on full-scale
plaster model of torso in Norway

229.

Page 132   Dedication of *The Spirit of Detroit*, September 23, 1958

230.

The Spirit of Detroit

1958, bronze and gilt bronze, 16 feet, in front of marble sculptural wall with *Seal of the City of Detroit* and *Seal of Wayne County*, diameter (each) 10 feet, City-County Building (now the Coleman A. Young Municipal Center), Detroit, Harley, Ellington and Day, architects

231.

Birth of the Atomic Age

1959, aluminum, 7³/₄ feet (fountain: marble and granite), National Exchange Club, Toledo, Ohio, Bellman, Gillette and Richards, architects

232.

Mercury

1960, polished nickel, 20 inches, Benson Ford Research Center, Henry Ford Museum and Greenfield Village, Dearborn, Michigan

Commissioned by the Mercury Division of Ford Motor Company to herald the announcement of the 1960 Mercury.

233.

Rendition of the *Great Seal of the United States*

1960, aluminum, diameter 6 feet, American Embassy, London, England

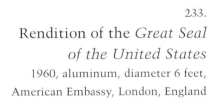

234.

Christ on the Cross
1959, small-scale model, Plasteline, 36 inches
(wooden cross: 84 inches), Indian River Catholic
Shrine, Indian River, Michigan

*I believe that to be great a work of art must
be more than just an exercise or experiment in
some material or medium. It must be above a
mere selfish satisfaction or desire for attention
and must have a true spiritual and emotional
content that has a constructive meaning for others.*

*That is why I am so grateful for the opportu-
nities I have to produce my work in a religious
theme, for while it is probably the most difficult
form of art it has the great blessing of returning
us again to a noble and dignified way of thinking
and causes us to again realize the greatness of
God and the unalterable fact that of ourselves
we can do nothing but that any talent or ability
we may have is an expression of Him.*
—MMF, excerpt from "The Opportunity in
Ecclesiastical Art," undated manuscript,
MFSM archives.

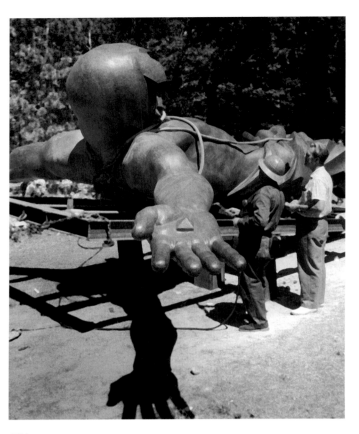

235.

Christ on the Cross
full-scale Plasteline and small-scale plaster
models of head and torso, in New York studio

236.
Welding and chasing of arms to torso, on site

237.

Christ on the Cross (detail)
1959

238.

Christ on the Cross
1959, bronze, 28 x 20 feet
(redwood cross: 55 x 22
feet), Indian River Catholic
Shrine (Cross in the Woods),
Indian River, Michigan

239.

Flying Pterodactyls

1960, plaster, head to tail: 92 inches; wingspan:
137 inches, MFSM

240.

Flying Pterodactyls

View from the reptile museum.

241.

Flying Pterodactyls

1960, bronze on granite, 16 feet
including base, Holden Museum
of Living Reptiles, Detroit
Zoological Institute, Royal Oak,
Michigan, Charles N. Agree,
architect

242–244.

Playground Equipment

c. 1960s, design proposals, stainless steel and
reinforced fiberglass, MFSM

Slide (below), climbing tree (right), and playhouse
(below right)

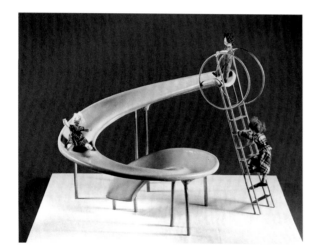

245.

*Nordic Swan and
the Ugly Duckling:
Hans Christian Andersen Fountain*
1962, bronze on limestone, 14 feet,
Danish Village, Rochester Hills, Michigan,
Edward Laird, landscape architect

246.

Nordic Swan

bronze, 38 inches

247.

Ugly Ducking

bronze, 10 inches

248.

Sculptured Clock and *Night and Day Fountain*

Henry J. McMorran Auditorium, Port Huron, Michigan

Alden B. Dow, architect

249.
Night, female figure from
Night and Day Fountain
1962, Plasteline, 14 feet long

250.
Night, female figure from
Night and Day Fountain
c. 1962, sketch model, bronze,
15 inches long, private collection

251.
Detail of *Day*
Plasteline

252.

Day, male figure from
Night and Day Fountain
1962, plaster, 14 feet long, MFSM

253–254.

Night and Day Fountain
1962, bronze, each figure 14 feet long,
Henry J. McMorran Auditorium, Port Huron, Michigan

255.

Sculptured Clock
1960, gold anodized aluminum, diameter 20 feet

The clock and auditorium were completed two
years prior to the fountain's installation, but the
project was conceived as a whole.

256.

Christ and the Children

1962, Plasteline model for aluminum relief, 6 feet,
commissioned for St. John's Lutheran Church,
Fort Wayne, Indiana

257.

Christ the Good Shepherd
1965, gold anodized aluminum, 18 feet,
Central United Methodist Church,
Waterford, Michigan

258.

Siberian Ram
1963, one of two limestone
carvings, 33 1/4 inches,
Baldwin Public Library,
Birmingham, Michigan, and
MFSM (originally at artist's
residence)

259.
Fredericks working on full-scale Plasteline model of *The Expanding Universe*, for the Department of State Building, Washington, D.C., 1964

Left: plaster and metal sketch model, 18 inches; right: quarter-scale plaster model. Both models are in the collection of the MFSM.

260.
Full-scale plaster section of figure from
The Expanding Universe

261.
View of the fountain from inside the
Department of State Building

262.
Nickel orbit: diameter 16 feet;
plaster sphere in background:
diameter 10 feet

263.

The Expanding Universe Fountain

1964, figure and sphere: bronze; orbit: nickel; basin: ceramic tile, 26 feet, South Court, Department of State Building, Washington D.C., Graham, Anderson, Probst and White, Inc., architects, in association with Harley, Ellington, Cowin and Stirton

The theme was selected to represent this age of great interest, exploration and discovery in outer space. The complete concept is intended to symbolize the vitality, order and mystery of the universe. The monumental central figure suggests a superhuman mythological being. He is seated upon a ten-foot sphere, encrusted with a multitude of stars of various magnitudes set in a pattern of the principal constellations of the celestial system. In his hands he holds two planets, which he is sending off into space. His hair, designed with jagged lightning-like forms, is studded with clusters of multi-pointed stars. The dynamic spiral orbit form swirling around the sphere represents the speed and perpetual movement of the heavenly bodies in space. Play of the water from numerous star-shaped sprays in a spiral pattern upon the figure, sphere, and orbit is intended to increase the feeling of movement.

—MMF, from a manuscript in artist's papers, MFSM archives.

Plate 1

Portrait of Lisa Sullivan McVey
1930, oil on canvas, 22 x 18 inches, MFSM

Plate 2

Birches
1934, pencil and watercolor on paper,
14 x 10 inches, private collection

Plate 3
Gru and Ega with Dinosaurs
c. 1935, pencil and watercolor on board,
14³/₈ x 18¹/₄ inches, MFSM

Plate 4
Gru and Ega with Giant Primates
c. 1935, pencil and watercolor on board,
15 x 20 inches, private collection

Paintings for a proposed children's book entitled
Gru and Ega: A Story of Evolution.

Plate 5
Mountains
1937, watercolor on paper, 14$\frac{1}{2}$ x 9 inches,
private collection

Plate 6
India
c. 1945, watercolor and ink on paper,
5 ³/₄ x 6 ⁵/₈ inches, MFSM

Plate 7
India (mountain landscape)
1945, watercolor and ink on paper,
3 ³/₄ x 6 inches, private collection

Plate 8
Female portrait
n.d., tempera on board, 9 x 7 ³/₄ inches, private collection

Plate 9

Levi L. Barbour Memorial Fountain
1936, bronze on granite, 16 x 20 feet, Belle Isle,
Detroit, Michigan

Plate 10

Victory Eagle

1950, marble, 30 feet, Veterans Memorial Building
(now the UAW–Ford National Program Center),
Detroit, Michigan

Plate 11
Furniture for the great apes (climbing tree and abstract climbing form)
1955, reinforced fiberglass and stainless steel

Built for the Holden Amphitheater and Great Ape House, Detroit Zoological Institute, Royal Oak, Michigan (building replaced by a new primate center in the 1980s).

Plate 12
The Ford Empire
1956, repoussé and formed metals; copper, nickel, brass, stainless steel, and aluminum, plated with gold, zinc, and cadmium, 145 feet long, Henry and Edsel Ford Auditorium, Detroit, Michigan

Plate 13

Harlequins (Clown Musicians) and
Ballerina (above), *Orchestral Parade* (below)
1956, repoussé and formed metals; copper, nickel, brass,
stainless steel, and aluminum, plated with gold, zinc, and
cadmium, Henry and Edsel Ford Auditorium, Detroit,
Michigan

Plate 14

The Spirit of Detroit

1958, bronze and gilt bronze, 16 feet,
City-County Building (now the Coleman A. Young
Municipal Center), Detroit, Michigan

Plate 15
Family, torso, and orb from
The Spirit of Detroit, 1958

Plate 16
Christ on the Cross
1959, figure: bronze, 28 x 20 feet;
cross: redwood, 55 x 22 feet,
Indian River Catholic Shrine
(Cross in the Woods), Indian
River, Michigan

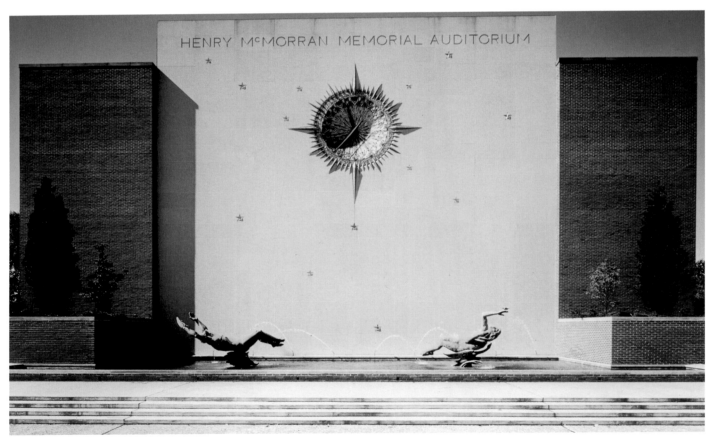

Plate 17
Night and Day Fountain and *Sculptured Clock*
Fountain figures: 1962, bronze, each 14 feet long; clock: 1960, gold
anodized aluminum, diameter 20 feet, Henry J. McMorran
Auditorium, Port Huron, Michigan

Plate 18

The Expanding Universe
1964, bronze and nickel, 26 feet, South Court,
Department of State Building, Washington, D.C.

Plate 19

Cleveland War Memorial: Fountain of Eternal Life
1964, figure and sphere: bronze, 46 feet; four carvings: Norwegian emerald-
pearl granite, 4 x 12 feet, Civic Center Mall A, Cleveland, Ohio

Plate 20
Fountain of Eternal Life at night

Plate 21

Saints and Sinners Fountain

1976, bronze on granite, 10 feet, Kresge Library,
Oakland University, Rochester, Michigan

Plate 22

Freedom of the Human Spirit
1986, 8 feet, Shain Park, Birmingham, Michigan

Originally created for the 1964 World's Fair in
New York, this casting was made in honor of the
city of Birmingham's 50th anniversary.

Plate 23
Sculpture garden at Fredericks's residence (*Leaping Gazelle* in foreground), Birmingham, Michigan, Wallace Frost, architect

Plate 24
Living room in Fredericks's residence (small-scale casting of Carl Milles's *Europa and the Bull* in foreground).

Plate 25
Wings of the Morning
1987, 56 x 53 inches, bronze, Brookgreen Gardens,
Pawleys Island, South Carolina

Plate 26
Pterodactyls, Female Baboon, Male Baboon,
and *Youth in the Hands of God*
1988, rear entrance, MFSM

Plate 27
Night (from Night and Day Fountain),
The Lion and Mouse, and *Two Sisters*
1988, Sculpture Garden, MFSM

Plate 28
Interior, Marshall M. Fredericks
Sculpture Museum, 1988

Plate 29
Lovesick, Acrobat, and *Juggler Clowns*
1991, bronze, 10 feet 7 inches, 14 feet, and 12 feet 4$^1/_2$ inches,
respectively, Frederik Meijer Gardens and Sculpture Park,
Grand Rapids, Michigan. Lena Meijer Conservatory in background.

Plate 30
The Friendly Dragon (one of two)
1991, bronze, 12 feet, Frederik Meijer
Gardens and Sculpture Park, Grand Rapids,
Michigan

Plate 31

Star Dream Fountain

1997, bronze, black granite, and stainless steel, 38 feet,

Barbara Hallman Plaza, Royal Oak, Michigan

Plate 32
Fredericks in his studio, 1998

And let the beauty of the Lord our God be upon us:
and establish thou the work of our hands upon us;
yea, the work of our hands establish thou it.
Psalm 90:17

264.
Fredericks with Plasteline model of
American Eagle (Victory Eagle), 1964

265.
American Eagle
1964, anodized aluminum, 21 feet,
John Weld Peck Federal Building,
Cincinnati, Ohio

266.
Indian
1964, Plasteline, 16 feet

267.
Swan
plaster, 9 x 8 feet, MFSM

268.
Indian and Wild Swans
1964, bronze, 35 feet, Milwaukee
Public Museum, Milwaukee,
Wisconsin, Eschweiller and Sielaff,
architects

270.

Male from *Freedom of the Human Spirit*
Plasteline; plaster sections of female at left

269.

Freedom of the Human Spirit
1964, small-scale model, bronze, 28 inches,
private collection

Models for work commissioned for the United
States Pavilion at the 1964 New York World's Fair,
Flushing Meadow, New York

271.

Female from *Freedom of the Human Spirit*
Plasteline; torso and head of male at left

272–273.

Freedom of the Human Spirit
1964, bronze, 27 feet, commissioned for the United
States Pavilion at the 1964 New York World's Fair,
Flushing Meadow, New York

Selected for permanent placement at the site of the
World's Fair, Flushing Meadow-Corona Park, New York.

*I tried to take the male and female figures and free
them from the earth. The only reason they stand up
in the space at all is because they are suspended by
sort of semi-visible abstract forms that keep them in
the air, and then there are three giant wild swans
flying with them. The idea was that these human
beings, these people—us, do not have to be limited to
the earth, to the ground. We can free ourselves men-
tally and spiritually whenever we want to, if we just
try to do so.*
—MMF, from *Marshall Fredericks: Spirit in Sculpture*
(videotaped interview), 1987.

274.

Cleveland War Memorial Fountain
1947, early drawing submitted to the Fine Arts Committee of the City Planning Commission, Cleveland, location unknown

275.
Site model for proposed *Cleveland War Memorial (Peace Memorial)*
1947, mixed media, 15 x 61³/₄ x 97¹/₂ inches, MFSM

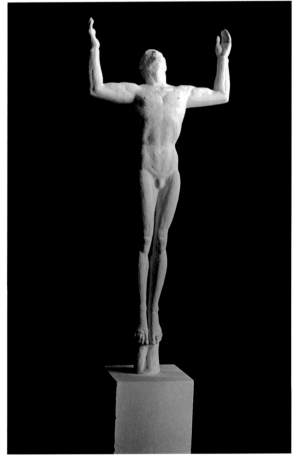

276.
Preliminary study for male figure, "Peace," for Cleveland War Memorial
1947, plaster, 29 inches, MFSM

277.
Fredericks working on *Peace Arising from the
Flames of War*, central figure for the *Cleveland
War Memorial: Fountain of Eternal Life*
c. 1949, quarter-scale Plasteline model, 12¹/₂ feet

Final selection for central figure, surrounded by
small-scale plaster models of project pieces.

278.
Final design, in Plasteline, for central figure
of the *Cleveland War Memorial*
1949

279.

Sphere for base of central figure for the
Cleveland War Memorial
Plasteline model for filigreed bronze, 10$^1/_2$ feet

Alternate view

The design contains symbols for Eternal Life, Spirit, and
Dominion, derived from ancient myths and legends.

280.

Southern Civilization
c. 1955, plaster model for carved granite, 4 x 12 feet,
location unknown

281.

Western Civilization
c. 1955, plaster model for carved granite, 4 x 12 feet,
location unknown

282.
Peace Arising from the Flames of War central figure for the *Cleveland War Memorial: Fountain of Eternal Life*, plaster, 46 feet

283.
Installation of *Cleveland War Memorial*, 1964

284.
Aerial view of the *Cleveland War Memorial: Fountain of Eternal Life*, 1945–64, Civic Center Mall A, Cleveland, Ohio

285.

Southern Civilization (African gods)
Norwegian emerald-pearl granite, 4 x 12 feet

286.

Western Civilization (Greek gods)
Norwegian emerald-pearl granite, 4 x 12 feet

287.

Nordic Civilization (Thor and other Nordic gods)
Norwegian emerald-pearl granite, 4 x 12 feet

288.

Eastern Civilization (gods of the Far East)
Norwegian emerald-pearl granite, 4 x 12 feet

289.

Cleveland War Memorial:
Fountain of Eternal Life
1964, figure and sphere: bronze, 46 feet;
surrounded by four carvings: Norwegian
emerald-pearl granite, 4 x 12 feet, Civic
Center Mall A, Cleveland, Ohio

Commissioned 1945, groundbreaking 1955,
dedicated on Memorial Day 1964.

The Lord is a sun and shield.
No man can shut that door.
All that God imparts moves in accord with Him.
One infinite God, good, governs.
He hath promised Eternal Life.
I give unto them Eternal Life.
That ye may know that ye have Eternal Life.
In hope of Eternal Life.
This is Life Eternal that they might know Thee.
Should not perish, but have Eternal Life.
As for me, I will behold Thy face in righteousness.
I shall be satisfied when I awake with Thy likeness.
For with Thee is the Fountain of Life.
—Compiled references from biblical passages in
Psalms, Revelation, the Gospel of John, I John and
Science and Health by Mary Baker Eddy, cited by the
artist as inspiration for the *Cleveland War Memorial.*

Page 159

290.
Fredericks standing with *Chief Pontiac*, 1964,
plaster model for gold anodized aluminum,
20 feet, commissioned for Community Bank
Pontiac, Michigan, James J. Morrison, architect (now the 30 North Building)

291.

The Princess and the Unicorn
1965, small-scale Plasteline study for large
fountain, 26¹/₂ inches, never enlarged to full-scale

292.

The Princess and the Unicorn
1965, bronze, 26¹/₂ inches, Starr Commonwealth,
Albion, Michigan

293.

Two Bears
1965, small-scale model, plaster,
16 inches, MFSM

294.
Fredericks working on full-scale
Plasteline model of *Two Bears*

I don't think you can be around children without them inspiring you and giving you ideas, and criticizing what you do. I think children are the greatest audience there is. They are most appreciative; they have a sense of humor and they like things. They don't have to be told what things are, they interpret them so readily themselves. They enjoy things so much more than many adults who are a little afraid to enjoy maybe. That's why they touch things and so on, because they like to enjoy every part of these things—the tactile quality as well as the visual.
—MMF, from *Marshall Fredericks: Spirit in Sculpture* (videotaped interview), 1987.

295.

Two Bears

1965, bronze, 6 feet 11 inches, private collection

Originally created for Lincoln Square, Urbana, Illinois, Victor Gruen, architect

296.

Industry and Other
Employment Activities
1965, aluminum, 14 feet long

Four reliefs for Ohio Bureau of Employment
Services and Ohio Department of Transportation,
Columbus, Ohio

297.
Recreational Activities
Plasteline model for aluminum relief

298.
Motion in Nature

299.
Transportation by Man

300.

Two Sisters Fountain
(Mother and Child)
1965, bronze, 5 feet, Kingswood School,
Cranbrook Educational Community,
Bloomfield Hills, Michigan (for plaster
model, see fig. 94)

301.

Flying Gulls Fountain

1968, aluminum on granite, 16 feet, Civic
Center and Loutit District Library Plaza,
Grand Haven, Michigan

302.

Wings of the Morning

1969, plaster model for bronze commissioned for
Kalamazoo Presbyterian Church, Kalamazoo, Michigan,
24 inches, MFSM (for full-scale bronze, see fig. 319)

If I take the wings of the morning, and dwell
    in the uttermost parts of the sea;
Even there shall thy hand lead me, and thy
    right hand shall hold me.
—Psalm 139: 9–10

Reverse view of plaster model

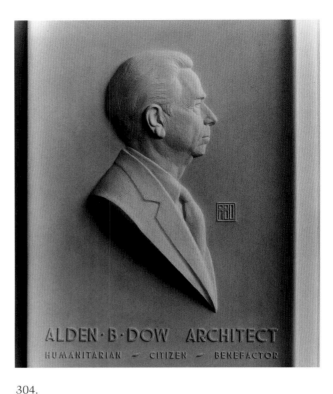

303.
William John Stapleton, Jr., M.D.
1970, plaster model for commissioned bronze relief for the
Shiffman Medical Library, Wayne State University, Detroit,
Michigan, 23 inches, MFSM

304.
Alden B. Dow
1970, plaster model for commissioned bronze relief
for Interlochen Center for the Arts, Interlochen,
Michigan, 36 x 31½ inches, MFSM

305.
Fredericks with *Sir Winston Churchill
Memorial*, 1967, Plasteline, 38 inches,
commissioned by the Grand Bahama Port
Authority, Freeport, Grand Bahama Island

306.

John F. Kennedy Memorial
1970, bronze on granite, 4$\frac{1}{2}$ feet on 6-foot
pedestal, Macomb County Building,
Mount Clemens, Michigan

307.
Victory Eagle (American Eagle)
1972, Plasteline, 12 feet

308.
Victory Eagle (American Eagle)
1972, bronze, 12 feet, Federal Reserve Bank, Cincinnati, Ohio, Harry Hake, architect

309.
The Friendly Frog
1970, polished green terrazzo with gold-plated bronze eyes, 5 x 8 feet, originally designed for Genesee Valley Plaza, Flint, Michigan, Louis Redstone, architect

Relocated to Flint Children's Museum.

310.

Persephone (Bacchante)
1972, bronze, 6 feet, Greek Theatre,
Cranbrook Educational Community,
Bloomfield Hills, Michigan

311.

Persephone (Bacchante)
1972, plaster, 6 feet, MFSM

Enlarged from Persephone
(Bacchante), small-scale model, 1932
(see fig. 23)

312.

Childhood

1975, Plasteline, 27 x 48 inches

313.

Henry Ford

1975, small-scale plaster model of
central figure for Henry Ford
Memorial, 26 inches, MFSM

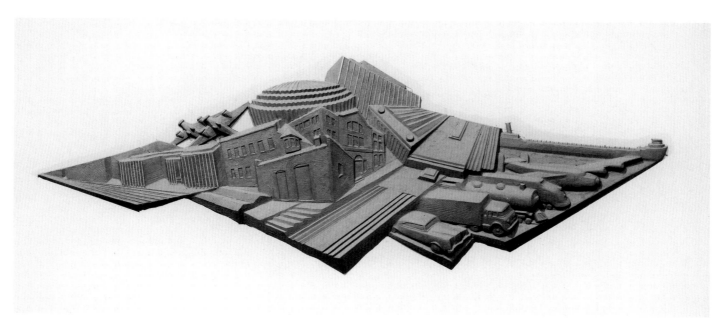

314.

The Ford Empire

1975, Plasteline, 27 x 48 inches

315.

Henry Ford Memorial

1975, bronze on marble, 11 x 16 feet; Ford figure: 73 inches; reliefs: 27 x 48 inches,
Henry Ford Centennial Library, Dearborn, Michigan

Historical reliefs depict events in Henry Ford's life; upper left, *Childhood*, lower
left, *Formative Years*, upper right, *The Ford Empire*, lower right, *Ford Cars*.

316.

Saints and Sinners Fountain

1976, bronze on polished granite, 10 feet, Kresge
Library, Oakland University, Rochester, Michigan

Enlarged from Saints and Sinners, 1939 (fig. 71)

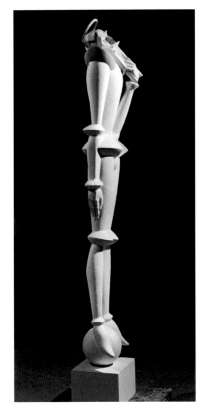

317.

Warrior Saint

Enlarged from Saints and Sinners, 1939
(see fig. 72), plaster, 10 feet, MFSM

318.

Black Elk: Homage to the Great Spirit
1980, small-scale model, plaster, 15³/₄ inches, MFSM
(for full-scale Plasteline model, see fig. 355)

Originally created to support the Tower of the Four Winds,
Black Elk Neihardt Park, Blair, Nebraska.

The Peace Pipe points from the Heart of Man to the Heart of God.
Black Elk prays through tears, "Oh, make my people live."

319.

Wings of the Morning
1987, bronze, 56 x 53 inches, Columbarium, Kirk in the Hills Presbyterian Church, Bloomfield Hills, Michigan

Enlarged from 1969 small-scale model (see fig. 302).

320.
Wings of the Morning, view from the Columbarium

Animal Kingdoms
1987, enlarged from 1939 sketches (see figs. 67–70), MFSM

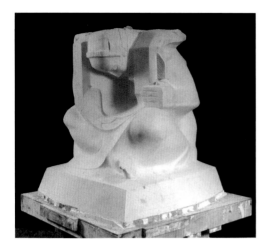

321.
Fish
plaster, 53 inches, MFSM

322.
Bird
plaster, 52 inches, MFSM

323.
Reptile
Plasteline, 55 inches

Small-scale plaster model in foreground, MFSM

324.
Mammal
plaster, 51¹/₂ inches, MFSM

325.
The Marshall M. Fredericks Sculpture Museum, Saginaw Valley State
University, University Center, Michigan, Ralph Calder and Associates Inc.,
architects, dedicated May 15, 1988

View from the sculpture garden, *Night and Day Fountain* in foreground.

326.
The Marshall M. Fredericks
Sculpture Museum, interior view

327–328.
The Marshall M.
Fredericks Sculpture
Museum, interior views

329.
Floyd Starr
1990, bronze, 31 inches, Starr Commonwealth,
Albion, Michigan

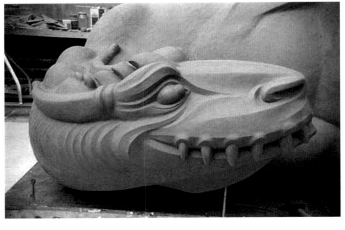

330.

The Friendly Dragon

1991, Plasteline, 12 feet, MFSM

Enlarged from 11-inch-long 1979 plaster scale model.

Detail of reverse

331.

The Friendly Dragon
(one of two)
1991, bronze, 12 feet, Frederik
Meijer Gardens and Sculpture
Park, Grand Rapids, Michigan

332.
Fredericks working on *Acrobat Clown*
1991, plaster, 14 feet, MFSM

Enlarged from 1938 scale model (see fig. 61).

333.
Lovesick Clown with *Acrobat Clown* and
Juggler Clown reflected against brick wall
1991, bronze, 10 feet 7 inches, 14 feet, and
12 feet 4^1/$_2$ inches, MFSM

334.
Three versions of *Siberian Ram*: full-scale plaster, 34 inches; original small-scale plaster (1941), 22 inches; and Plasteline reduction (1996), 9 inches, plaster models located at MFSM

Limited edition bronzes of the 1996 reduction were cast for a Capital Commemorative Campaign to benefit the Marshall M. Fredericks Sculpture Museum, beginning in 1999.

335.
Marshall Fredericks with *Siberian Ram* 1993, bronze, 34 inches, Renaissance Center People Mover Station, Detroit

Bronze version of 1963 limestone carving (see fig. 258).

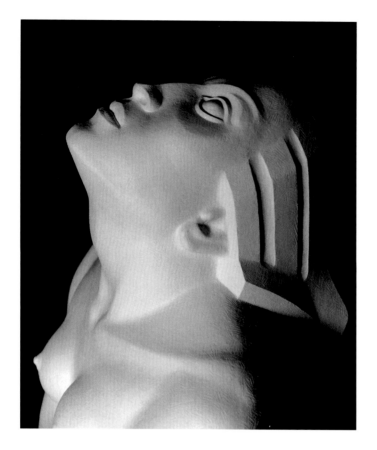

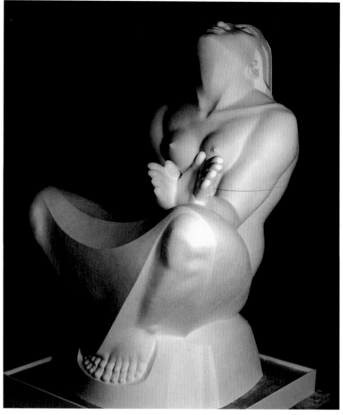

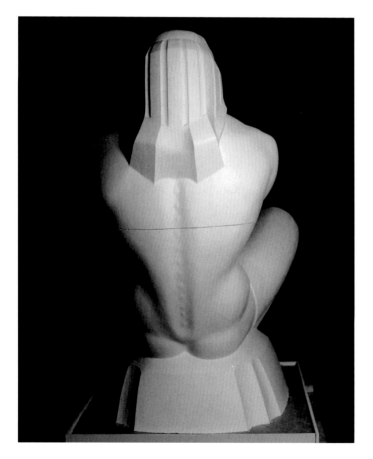

336.

Sun Worshipper

1994, plaster, 69 inches, MFSM

Enlarged from 1937 small-scale model (see fig. 41).
The full-scale bronze casting is in a private collection.

337.
God on the Rainbow
Full-scale Plasteline models of *God* and *Angel*

338.
Fredericks working on Plasteline model of
God for *God on the Rainbow*, 1995

Based on a 1946 sketch by Carl Milles
for a peace monument intended for the
United Nations Building in New York,
Fredericks's enlargement now stands
at the entrance to Stockholm Harbor,
a project spearheaded by Cilla Jahn, in
collaboration with Millesgården and
the AP Foundation.

339.
Sketch models for *God on the Rainbow*

340.
Angel
1995, bronze, 7 feet

341.
The angel Gabriel throws
stars up to God who hangs
them on Heaven's arch.

342.

God on the Rainbow (Gud Fader På Himmelsbågen)
1995, God figure: bronze: 12 feet 4 inches; angel figure: bronze,
7 feet; rainbow arc: stainless steel, 69 feet, Nacka Strand, Sweden

343.
Baboon Playing a Mandolin
1996, Plasteline, 56 inches

Enlarged from 1939 small-scale plaster model
shown at left (for 1939 bronze, see fig. 75).

344.
Baboon Playing a Mandolin
1996, plaster, 56 inches, MFSM

345.

Baboon Playing a Mandolin and *Baboon and Baby Chimpanzee* in the "Greenhouse" studio, 1996, plaster, 56 and 58¼ inches, MFSM

Bronze castings of these two works are in the children's garden, Community House, Birmingham, Michigan.

346.

Baboon and Baby Chimpanzee
1996, bronze, 58¼ inches, Frederik Meijer Gardens and Sculpture Park, Grand Rapids, Michigan

347.

Star Dream Fountain
1997, bronze, granite, and stainless steel, 38 feet,
Barbara Hallman Plaza, Royal Oak, Michigan

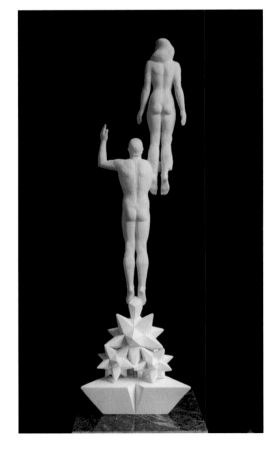

348.

Star Dream Fountain
1997, small-scale model, plaster,
38¹/₂ inches, MFSM

349.
Fredericks working on full-scale Plasteline model of male figure for *Star Dream Fountain*, 1997

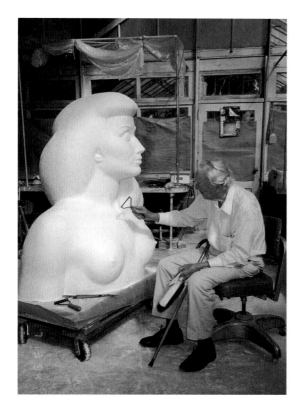

350–351.
Fredericks working on sections of full-scale plaster model of female figure for *Star Dream Fountain*, 1997

Complete full-scale plaster model located at MFSM.

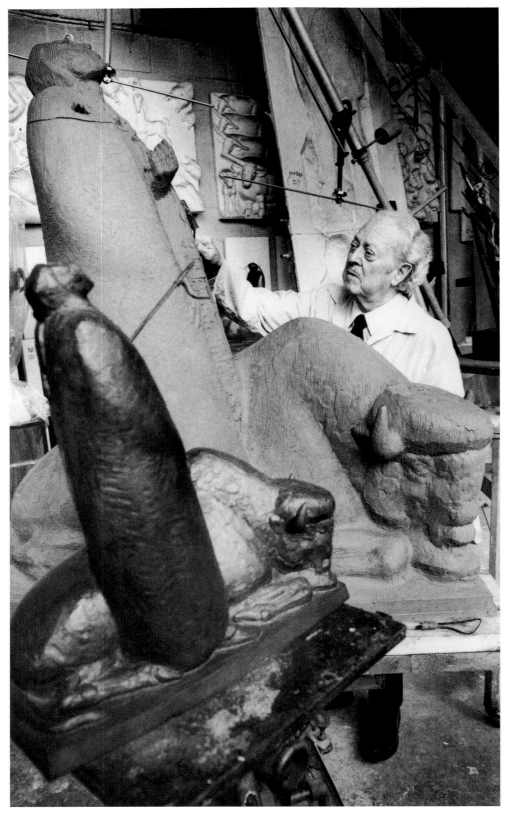

352.
Fredericks working on Plasteline inter-
mediate scale model of *Black Elk*, with
small-scale model, 1998

353.

Black Elk

1998, bronze, 12 feet 4 inches, Sterling Bank and Trust,
Southfield, Michigan

View on-site of patination at Bedi-Makky Foundry,
New York.

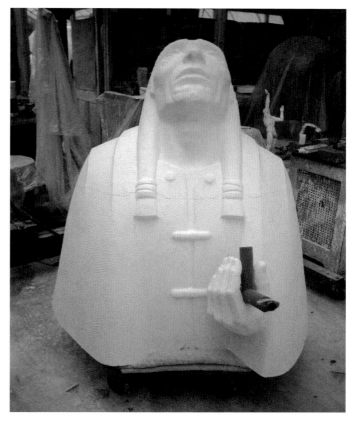

354.

Black Elk

1998, plaster, MFSM

355.
Fredericks with *Black Elk: Homage to the Great Spirit*, 1998, Plasteline, 12 feet 4 inches, enlarged from small-scale model, 1980 (see fig. 318)

Then I was standing on the highest moun-tain of them all, and round beneath me was the whole hoop of the world. And while I stood there I saw more than I can tell and I understood more than I saw; for I was seeing in the sacred manner the shapes of all things in the spirit, and the shape of all shapes as they must live together like one being. And I saw that the sacred hoop of my people was one of the many hoops that made one circle, wide as daylight and as starlight, and in the center grew one mighty flowering tree to shelter all the children of one mother and one father.

—"Peace" from *Black Elk Speaks* by John G. Neihardt, noted by Fredericks as inspiration for Black Elk

356.
Fredericks working on Plasteline model of *Lord Byron*,
1998, 12 feet

The artist's last monumental work was cast in bronze
one year after his death, for installation at the Marshall
M. Fredericks Sculpture Museum.

I have spent so much time tuning my harp
that I have not sung the songs I came to sing.
—source unknown

357.
Marshall Fredericks with guests at the
opening of museum, 1988

The Marshall M. Fredericks Sculpture Museum

"Those who create beauty from stone will live forever."
—From an ancient Greek source

T he museum dedicated to the life and work of Marshall M. Fredericks is housed in an award-winning thirty-foot-tall glass and marble building,[1] located in the Arbury Fine Arts Center at Saginaw Valley State University (SVSU), in University Center, Michigan (see figs. 358–359). One of the few comprehensive collections of a single artist's works in the world and one of a small number of American museums exclusively devoted to the work of a single sculptor (among the others so honored are Isamu Noguchi, Daniel Chester French, and Augustus Saint-Gaudens), the ten-thousand-square-foot facility opened to the public on May 15, 1988. Over a thousand original plaster models, cast and carved sculptures of various sizes—from monumental to miniature—and medals created during his six-decade-long career illustrate the genius and bravura of Fredericks's artistic achievement. The impressive collection donated by Fredericks and his wife Rosalind also includes drawings, photographs, armatures, site and sketch models, molds, tools, memorabilia, and over one hundred linear feet of archives containing correspondence, project files, contracts, and other materials related to his life and work. It is awe-inspiring to visit the museum and realize that a single individual created so many sculptures during his lifetime.

The extraordinary harmony of the museum's design and its contents demonstrates Fredericks's belief in the inextricable interrelationship of sculpture and architecture. Not only did he work with the architects to determine the placement of his sculptures and the arrangement of the windows for optimum lighting, he was also instrumental in choosing the museum's color scheme and the interior materials. As a result, all the elements work together as a whole, truly reflecting the sculptor's own vision. The quality of light entering the museum changes throughout the day, enhancing the three-dimensionality of the sculptures. In the great gallery, sunlight reflects off the highly polished travertine walls and floors, illuminating the white plaster models and creating an unexpected contrast of monochrome colors and finishes that take on opposing roles. Though their surfaces are matte, the plasters appear luminescent against the floors and walls. During the day the plasters are silhouetted against the light from the large windows, while at night their mirrored images reflect back from the glass. The large windows also serve to make the sculptures in the exterior garden visible from the gallery's interior during the day, and conversely allow the interior works to be seen from outside in the evening. In the reception area, large photographic wall panels and period photographs of the finished pieces in their original placements, the artist in his studio sculpting clay or posing with his plaster models grace the wall to the left of the entrance (fig. 361). Other displays exhibit his tools and demonstrate the process of sculptural creation—from conception in the artist's mind to the finished work. Bronze casts, donated by individual museum supporters, grace a reflective pool and are interspersed throughout the museum's sculpture garden, campus walkways, and a plaza with a central fountain. A visit to the museum is a holistic experience, a constant interplay of architecture and art.

358.
Architectural rendering by Hideo Fujii of schematic design
for the Marshall M. Fredericks Sculpture Museum,
Ralph Calder and Associates, Inc., architects, Detroit, c. 1984

359.
Arbury Fine Arts Center and Marshall M.
Fredericks Sculpture Museum, 1988

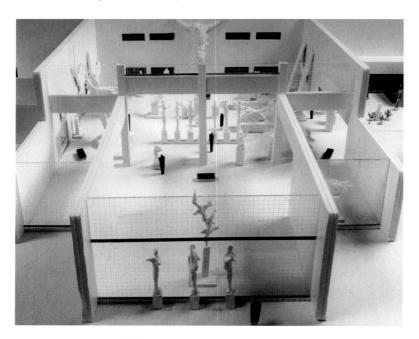

360.
Architectural model with scale mock-ups
positioned by Fredericks

The Marshall M. Fredericks Sculpture Museum exists because of the artist's friendship with Ned and Dorothy (Honey) Arbury. In the 1930s Honey was a student of Fredericks at the Cranbrook Academy of Art, and in the 1960s both the Arburys became reacquainted with Fredericks and his wife Rosalind through Honey's uncle, Alden B. Dow. Dow, a well-known and accomplished Michigan architect, was a dear friend and contemporary of Fredericks and had also collaborated on several projects with him. The Arburys were long-standing and dedicated supporters of SVSU, and it was Honey's idea that a museum devoted to Fredericks's work should be created and made a part of the school's planned fine arts center. While traveling with Fredericks and his wife in Europe, she and Ned persuaded him to consider the idea. On February 27, 1980, Fredericks sent a letter to Jack Ryder, then president of SVSU, saying that if the university could incorporate proper housing and safekeeping of his collection into the plans being developed for the fine arts center, he and his wife would consider designating SVSU as the collection's permanent repository. Within a month of his inquiry, the university conferred upon Fredericks an honorary doctorate and presented him with an architectural concept for a museum gallery devoted to his works.

The creation of the Arbury Fine Arts Center and the Marshall M. Fredericks Sculpture Museum was the culmination of several parallel stories. While it brought to fruition the vision of the Arburys, it was also the realization of the dreams of both the university and Marshall Fredericks. The administration believed that a museum devoted to Fredericks's work would inspire students studying the fine arts, provide cultural enrichment for all the students, faculty, and staff at the university, and attract visitors and scholars not only from Michigan and the United States but also from throughout the world.

For Fredericks, it was an opportunity to play a direct role in the creation of a museum dedicated to his works and a way to preserve his legacy. He repeatedly referred to the museum as a "miracle in a bean field," because the museum and the university grew up out of farmland, close to the Tri-Cities of Saginaw, Midland, and Bay City. By the time this project was initiated, Fredericks, lacking enough room to store them, had already destroyed eighty percent of his original plasters. The plasters that remained at his studio in Royal Oak and at the "Greenhouse" in Bloomfield Hills, and the hundred pieces of Christ on the Cross that had been stored in a semi-open shed in Norway for twenty-five years are a part of this miracle. It took Fredericks and his assistants Molly Barth and Scott Slocum over nine years to restore and repair these plasters before their eventual transfer to SVSU, where they were finally installed with help from Tom Pallazzolo, Richard Novak, Bob Devers, and Jon Kinney.

The university had long planned for additional instructional space for music and the visual arts, and the 1978 master plan for the campus included the envisioned art center. Following the agreement with Fredericks, the architects, Ralph Calder and Associates, Inc., of Detroit, incorporated the museum into the conceptual plans for the art center.

Preliminary plans were developed in March 1980 by design architect Hideo H. Fujii and project manager Dennis C. Anderson, and in July 1980 the university design team, which included the Frederickses, visited the Henry Moore Gallery at the Art Gallery of Ontario in Toronto because it was built to display plaster models. While developing the schematic design, the team consulted with other museum professionals at the Saint-Gaudens National Historic Site in Cornish, New Hampshire, and at the Detroit Institute of Arts. Throughout the process Fredericks worked closely with the architects in developing the detailed plans for the museum. Using the architectural model of the museum, he made scale mock-ups of his works to determine their placement and plan their installation (fig. 360).

In 1984, having already raised nearly a million dollars toward a projected cost of seven million dollars for the art center and museum (which included a $380,000 grant from the state of Michigan), the university began a public capital campaign. By December of the first year five million dollars had been raised from 260 donors, including individuals,

361.

The Thinker sits outside the gallery entrance beckoning visitors to enter.

362.
Installers positioning sections of the plaster model for *Nordic Civilization* from the *Cleveland War Memorial: Fountain of Eternal Life*

363–364.
Fredericks and the sculpture garden fountain during and after installation

corporations, and foundations. The ground-breaking ceremony took place in June 1986, and in that same month Fredericks entered into an agreement with the university wherein it was agreed that a ten-thousand-square-foot gallery for the exclusive display and storage of sculptures and other works by Fredericks would be established and that he would transfer works, models, and related artistic materials for display and use in the gallery. The agreement also allowed for the preparation, transportation, casting, transfer, and conveyance of sculptures that needed to occur before construction was completed, as all placements had to be carefully planned to avoid having to move sculptures multiple times, particularly those weighing several tons. In March 1988, after the marble interior walls were attached, but before the marble floors were installed, paper templates were taped on the walls to determine the height and position of reliefs and sculptures. Once the locations were confirmed, holes for the steel brackets and mounting supports were predrilled. It took three months to complete the gallery installation. Many of Fredericks's works are monumental in scale, and the engineering required to attach, secure, and support the plaster models required the assistance of many specialists and artisans (fig. 362). The first sculpture to be installed was the twenty-eight-foot-tall Christ figure on the south wall, which was mounted over a specially designed aluminum support to maintain its structural integrity. After everything was hung on the walls, the marble flooring was laid. The remaining sculptures were then installed and smaller works placed inside cases.

Somewhat incredibly, the construction of the Arbury Fine Arts Center and the Marshall M. Fredericks Sculpture Gallery (later changed to Museum) was completed in two years; it was dedicated on Sunday, May 15, 1988. Both the Arburys and Fredericks were honored at the dedication and opening ceremony with resolutions by the Michigan legislature The resolution honoring Fredericks read in part: "People who have the talent and creativity of Marshall M. Fredericks enrich our world. They have a vision that captivates us as we see their artistic creations, and they make our world a bit more beautiful. Marshall Fredericks has used this artistic flare and his deep understanding of life's meaning to fulfill his desire to give other people happiness."[2]

The museum's by-laws were adopted in October 1988, and a year later, following a national search, the museum's first director and curator, Michael W. Panhorst, was hired. Since its opening fourteen years ago, the museum has seen rapid increases in its attendance and now hosts over ten thousand local, national, and international visitors every year. It has also doubled the size of its collection. In 1992, the Frederickses established a fund for acquisition and conservation and an endowment for the preservation and conservation of sculptural and other artistic works. In 1994 the Rosalind C. Fredericks Educational Trust, an endowment named in honor of Mrs. Fredericks, was established to help increase attendance and to improve service through educational programming. A membership group, established in 1993, also contributes substantially to the museum's operational costs through annual appeals.

Fredericks never considered the museum completed. To him it was a living and growing space, and in the years before his death he gave the gallery additional plaster models. In 1996 he offered to donate the balance of his sculptural models, molds, drawings, and studio contents, including his business records to the museum. A 1996 agreement provided for an expansion of the museum, and once again Fredericks worked closely with the architect, Carl Roehling of the SmithGroup, Detroit, on the conceptual design. When the artist died in 1998 at the age of ninety, a $2.5 million capital campaign was already in progress to fund an approximately 8,600-square-foot addition to house his promised gift. The design for the expansion was revised in 2000 (designer: James Luckey; project manager: Ronald Omilian, both of the SmithGroup), and includes a gallery devoted to the sculptural process that will be installed to resemble Fredericks's

365.
Marshall Fredericks in the main gallery, south and west sides partially installed (note the tape on the floor, used to specify exact placement).

366.
Conceptual design for the gallery interior, Ralph Calder and Associates, Inc., architects, c. 1984

Rendering by Hideo Fujii.

Royal Oak studio, including his workbench and drafting table, tools, armatures, clay models, molds, and pointing devices. In addition there will be a temporary exhibition gallery, gallery for works on paper, a multi-purpose room that can serve as a studio for hands-on demonstrations and educational classrooms, an education court with interactive computers, an audiovisual presentation area, relocation of offices, an archives storage and study area, a preparator's clean room, and an expanded collections storage area (fig. 367).

Marshall Fredericks believed in humanitarian and civic involvement. He believed that art should enhance and beautify the lives of people and, therefore, should be in places where people in their daily living can see it and come to know it. As Samuel Sachs II, former director of the Detroit Institute of Arts and now director of the Frick Collection in New York, points out, few living artists get to see the effect of their legacy. No doubt fewer still have the satisfaction of seeing part of their legacy not only preserved but also put to such an inspiring and educational use.

EXISTING MUSEUM | MUSEUM ADDITION

MUSEUM ADDITION

ARBURY FINE ARTS CENTER

EXISTING MUSEUM

367.
Schematic design for Phase II museum expansion, SmithGroup Inc., 2002

Mrs. Jo Saltzman, chair of the SVSU Board of Control at the time of the museum's opening, eloquently described the contribution of the Arbury Fine Arts Center and the Marshall M. Fredericks Sculpture Museum to the university's mission. "Art," she remarked, "adds an extra dimension to enrich education, and ultimately life itself. It adds beauty and symmetry to the campus, it expands our ability to appreciate the subtle nuances of the physical world, and it challenges us to reexamine abstract ideas—social, political, and moral— which have been transformed through the artist's vision." The Marshall M. Fredericks Sculpture Museum instills that esthetic, while honoring one of the foremost twentieth-century figurative sculptors in the country.

—Barbara Heller

1. The MFSM won the Michigan Masonry Institute Award.

2. From Michigan House Concurrent Resolution 770-05-11-1988; Resolution 773-05-10-1988 cited the Arburys for their contributions not only to SVSU but to the state as a whole.

368.
Marshall Fredericks working on the
Cleveland War Memorial, 1946

The Sculpture Process

When Marshall Fredericks began his career as a sculptor, he faced a centuries-old path well-trodden by proven American masters of the art, such as Daniel Chester French, Augustus Saint-Gaudens, Gutzon Borglum, and Lorado Taft. Traditional methods that had been used for hundreds of years were the ones still practiced by sculptors to produce their work. The mainstays of a sculptor's tool belt were the old reliables: clay, wood, wax, plaster, marble, and bronze, and carving or modeling were the methods by which a sculptor created his work. Carvers worked directly in stone or wood, while modelers faced many intricate steps that led to a bronze version of an original clay. Fredericks used these time-tested methods but also expanded his repertoire to include new and untried materials as he matured in his work. To truly understand how he brought his ideas to life, it is helpful to have a grasp of these working methods. This chapter represents a brief overview of some of the processes he used in carrying out his work.

Sculpture may go through many stages before it reaches its final, permanent form. The actual process starts in a small way and with the simplest of tools: pencil and paper. Sketches give some visual semblance to an idea and provide direction for the ensuing clay model. If the work is designed for an architectural façade or for a particular location, the sculptor builds a scale model of the proposed building or site, including trees, adjacent buildings, and the proposed sculpture itself. This allows the sculptor to determine the correct height, size, and scale, the effect of changing light, and to examine the work's interrelationship with all surrounding elements. Once this important step is completed and approved, the traditional method of working up to a large sculpture is to incrementally enlarge the first model, generally created on a scale of one inch to a foot, first to a quarter-scale and then to a full-size clay version of the final piece.

The physical act of making sculpture now begins. The first clay model, or maquette, which can be between twelve and eighteen inches high, needs little support—perhaps a fixed wire or two, fastened to a shellacked board. Onto this wire support are pressed small pieces of a pliable, oil-based clay called Plasteline, which has the useful quality of not drying out and the ability to be reworked over long periods. It is with this small version that the sculptor has the most latitude to explore his idea in the round. Gesture, balance, proportion, whether the piece "says what he wants to say" are determined in this most critical period. When the original model is completed, the greater part of the creative process is done.

For the work ahead, the sculptor needs a more durable working model, so a plaster cast or copy must be made from the clay. To do this, a mold is taken by encasing the clay model in plaster of Paris, which is then hardened and the clay removed, producing a negative image. Next, a release agent, a soapy separator solution, is brushed into the cavity of the plaster mold to prevent the positive cast from adhering to the surface. Fresh plaster is poured into the mold. The outer plaster casting, or "waste" mold, is then carefully chipped away, leaving the inner plaster cast intact. The measurements to enlarge the piece to quarter scale will be taken from this model.

Creating a larger clay model involves more than just additional clay. The larger the work, the more necessary it is to have in place a sturdy structure to hold the weight of the additional material. This support, or armature, can be made of many different elements: steel rods, heavy wire, welded iron, wood, metal sheeting, whatever will hold the weight and stay put. For a

369.

Fredericks and an assistant enlarging *Warrior Saint*

sculpture with large surface areas, this underlying structure must be designed so that it will support a single layer of clay. One method, used by Fredericks, is to construct the main armature of sturdy pine posts and then to nail crosspieces of lathing onto this skeleton, leaving space enough between each lath so that the clay will squeeze between the pieces and not shift when weight is added to it. Building a solid armature from accurate measurements is crucial before beginning the enlargement process.

Enlarging the clay model demands very precise equipment, ranging from simple proportional calipers to the more sophisticated pantograph, or pointing machine. To use a pantograph machine, the sculptor takes a series of measurements for various key points on the small model, which are proportionately increased and transferred to the quarter-scale model. The pantograph machine consists of a long aluminum arm from which extend two pointers or rods at some distance apart, one to be positioned against the small plaster model and one to

extend toward the enlarged armature. Hundreds of tiny dots are made in pencil on the small plaster model, and when the first pointer touches one of these points, the other moves to the corresponding spot on the armature, indicating the "point" to which the clay must be built up. Returning to the small plaster model, the sculptor moves the pointer to the next dot and continues the process, revolving the turntables, upon which both models rest, until the large form emerges—an exact but larger copy of the small version.

The quarter-scale model provides another opportunity to define details. By the time the piece is ready to be enlarged to the full-scale size, all aspects of the sculpture have been worked out, and what remains is the physical effort of applying the clay layer to the larger form, now supported by a stronger armature, and creating the final texture. The piece is now ready for the plaster work.

There are three kinds of plaster casting: one uses a waste mold, another a piece mold (both plaster of Paris), and the third a gelatin or flexible rubber mold; all reproduce the original clay. The waste mold, previously described, is chipped away (wasted) to free the hardened cast, which was poured in as liquid plaster. The piece mold, which is divided into sections that can be pulled away from the cast intact, can be used again. The flexible or gelatin mold can with care be released from more delicate casts, removed intact, and used for replicas.

The complexity of making plaster molds increases with their size. In order for large molds to be taken apart without damage, they must be divided into sections. To create these sections, dividing walls, thin metal strips called shims, are pressed into the clay to delineate previously defined areas. Liquid plaster is thrown onto the clay surface of each of these sections and built up to an even thickness. When the plaster of one of these sections has hardened, the shims are removed, and a separator solution applied to the shim wall so that the next section will not stick to the first. The sculptor continues in this way, building up these adjacent mold sections until the entire clay model is completely encased by the mold. To increase the mold's strength and provide handles with which to lift the plaster sections from the clay model, aluminum rods, bent to follow the form, are embedded into the mold sections using plaster-soaked burlap strips. Once the plaster sections harden, they are pulled away from the clay and reassembled. To create the final full-scale plaster cast, a release agent is applied so that new plaster will not adhere to the mold, and an even layer of wet plaster is built up against this mold surface. If the piece is large, strengthening agents of burlap, rods, and pipe are positioned inside the positive plaster cast. When the inner cast has hardened, the outer mold sections are released and the sculptor has yet another opportunity to correct and refine the surface of his work, using special plaster tools designed for this purpose.

It is this completed full-size plaster model that is shipped, in sections if the piece is exceptionally large, to the foundry for casting. Bronze foundries are dirty, noisy, exciting places with their ovens, crucibles, cranes, casting pits, and electric grinding and welding machines. A sculptor spends a lot of time at the foundry, touching up the wax (if the lost-wax method is used), supervising welding operations, and overseeing the application of the patina, or final color. He greatly depends upon the knowledge and skill of the foundry professionals to reproduce well what he has so laboriously created. Fredericks used many foundries, including Fine Arts, Mengel, and Daedalus in Michigan, Bedi-Rassy, Bedi-Makky, Tallix, and Modern Art in New York, and Kristiana Kunst & Metalstøberi in Oslo, Norway, where his three most challenging commissions were cast: the *Christ on the Cross* in Indian River, Michigan (fig. 238), *The Spirit of Detroit* (fig. 230), and the *Cleveland War Memorial* (fig. 289). For a time, demands for his work made it necessary to keep three separate studios in operation, in Oslo, New York City, and Royal Oak, Michigan.

Most of Fredericks's larger sculptures were sand cast into bronze, a process more

370.
Assistant Thomas Marker with the armature for *American Eagle* (Ann Arbor War Memorial Eagle), 1949

371.
Fredericks working on the full-scale clay model of *American Eagle*, 1949

372.
Plaster mold sections for *American Eagle*, 1949

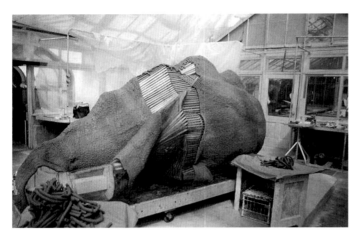

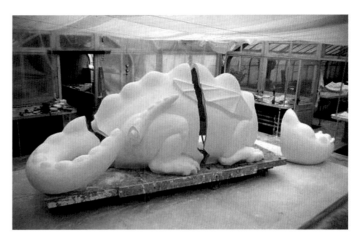

373.
The Friendly Dragon, showing armature, lathing, and
clay extrusions, 1991

374.
Full-scale plaster sections of *The Friendly Dragon*,
ready for the foundry, 1991

suitable than lost-wax casting for the smooth, simplified forms that so characterize his work. Sand casting differs from the lost-wax method in that the original plaster is packed in damp "French sand," a combination of clay, silica, and alumina, while encased in iron frames called flasks, individual sections that can be separated or bolted together as needed. The molder gently hammers the damp sand against the plaster model as it lies inside the flasks, filling all recesses and creating mold sections with the damp sand. When they have hardened, the sections are removed from the plaster cast, the plaster is lifted out, and the sand mold sections replaced within the flasks. A core is positioned inside allowing the final bronze cast to be hollow. The flasks are reassembled and bolted together, and the heated bronze is poured into the space vacated by the plaster model. After the bronze cools, the flasks are broken apart, the core tapped out, and the newly cast pieces welded together. The seams and rough edges are ground down or chased, and the patina, or coloring, is applied.

There are other ways of casting bronze. The lost-wax method, a process that is thousands of years old, involves taking a wax impression from a flexible rubber mold and producing a hollow wax version of the original model. To do this, hot wax is painted onto the surface of the mold, the thickness governed by the size of the sculpture to be

cast—usually no more than one quarter inch for a life-size figure. The wax positive is removed from the mold, and rods, or sprues, of wax are attached to vent trapped air and provide additional paths for the liquid bronze to travel. The hollow wax model is then coated with a liquid refractory material, looking very much like wet plaster, that is able to withstand temperatures up to 2000 degrees Fahrenheit when built up to a certain thickness, and allowed to harden. The hollow interior of the wax model is filled with a core of the same material, pins connecting the core to the outside shell are affixed, and the whole piece is placed in a furnace to allow the wax to melt out (thus, "lost wax") just prior to the pouring of the bronze. The liquid bronze now takes the place of the wax. Once the bronze cools, the refractory shell is knocked off, and the usual finishing work, welding, chasing, and patina application follows.

Patination, the final treatment, or coloring, of the bronze, is a complex science that requires much skill and experience. Left alone, bronze will age and acquire a certain look depending on its particular alloy make-up or its location—whether it is situated near seawater, subject to urban pollutants, or even buried underground. But it normally takes a long time for these elements to affect the metal. Sculptors and trained foundry men can speed up this process with a heat torch and liquid chemical formulas; the bronze surface is heated while layers of liquid chemicals are brushed or stippled onto the metal in random patterns. Formulas for these chemical compositions are closely guarded, and it takes many years to become a master of this important final step. But in the hands of a professional the procedure can produce the most beautiful effects in almost any color range. Fredericks became known for a particular green patina, which he chose for much of his work. There was extensive communication between his studios in the United States and the foundries in Europe regarding this coloring of his bronze sculpture. Fredericks sent his own formulas to Oslo to be tested for *The Spirit of Detroit* and the *Cleveland War Memorial*, and treated bronze samples would be sent back to him for testing and approval. Given the intricacies of the process, a sculptor must also be a scientist. Fredericks was familiar with the chemicals used for patination, including copper nitrate, liver of sulfur, copper sulfate, ammonium chloride, and nitric acid, to name just a few. Some of the equipment used in this process includes a gas torch, ventilation apparatus, copper-brass wire brushes, airbrush compressor, and face mask with chemical filters. After the chemicals have done their work, the bronze is fixed, or stabilized, by applying wax to the surface and then polished with a soft cloth.

Several of Fredericks's major works combine cast bronze with stone, and he was particularly attuned to the act of carving.

> When I am working in clay or carving, especially carving, I can isolate myself from everything. Unfortunately, I can't do it all the time, but I can isolate myself because I constantly think this is what the light will do, this is what the light won't do, this is what the positive form should do against the negative form, or this is what the sharp edge should do against the curved edge.
> —MMF, Marshall Fredericks: *Spirit in Sculpture* (videotaped interview), 1987

The sculptor's oeuvre includes works in other materials as well, some of them quite innovative. He was thoroughly trained in all branches of the sculptor's art, and his mastery of clay, plaster, stone, and resins, as well as bronze and other metals enabled him to draw from any of these materials when he designed his works. His favorite stone was Norwegian emerald-pearl granite, the material he chose for the powerful figures representing the four spiritual paths in his *Cleveland War Memorial Fountain* (figs. 285-288), each of which was carved from a block weighing ten tons. A coarse-grained igneous rock made up of crystals fused together over time by great pressure, granite is one of the hardest of stones. Softer stones such as marble or limestone are carved by slicing off bits of the surface. Granite, however, is "beaten" into the desired shape, the crystals must be broken and bruised by pounding down directly with heavy chisels and hammers. To accomplish his aims, Fredericks trained his Norwegian assistants in the necessary techniques— skills he had mastered as assistant to Carl Milles's chief stone carver. The Cleveland work was cast and finished in Norway, and the idea of polishing granite to a fine shine was new to Norwegian artisans—generally it would be left rough cut. So that the work could be completed as he had designed it, Fredericks brought his own stone polishing

375.
Single largest block of Vermont marble ever quarried at the time, nineteen tons, for *Victory Eagle*, Veterans Memorial Building, 1949

376.
Fredericks and assistant carving Norwegian emerald-pearl granite for the Cleveland War Memorial in Norway, c. 1963

377.
Fredericks directing the assembly of formed metal pieces for the Ford Auditorium mural, 1956. "I wanted it to be like a gigantic piece of jewelry."—MMF

tools to Norway and introduced this skill as well to his assistants, who then finished the job.

In Columbus, Ohio, Fredericks and two assistants executed, on site, six high reliefs in limestone on the front of the Ohio Union Building (fig. 169). The eight-foot-tall sculptures, reflecting the history of the Ohio River Valley, were carved in place, high up on scaffolding, which enabled the sculptor to calculate the effect of natural light on the relief and adjust the forms accordingly.

For his 145-foot-long mural *The Ford Empire* for the Henry and Edsel Ford Auditorium in Detroit, Michigan (fig. 213), Fredericks chose hammered, welded, and plated metals. At the time, the mural was the largest metal sculpture of its kind and took three years to complete. A separate studio had to be built and another space rented in order to accommodate the construction and assembly of the aluminum, brass, nickel, copper, and stainless steel pieces of the central span. Four skilled artisans were hired to assist with the work. The gleaming polished copper and brass theatrical designs on the two end walls were fashioned in repoussé, an ancient process in which a sculptural form is formed out of metal sheets using round headed hammers and metal punches. The forms are beaten into the sheets from the reverse side and then controlled and refined on the converse side. To complete the innovative approach, some of the mural and end-wall design surfaces were coated with clear baked enamel or plated with gold, cadmium, and zinc.

In 1953, Fredericks was the first sculptor to work in fiberglass, when he designed and fabricated sixteen eight-foot panels for the Ford Rotunda, representing the industries that contributed to the automobile industry (figs. 178–180). The commission called for the artwork to be designed in a lightweight, lasting material that could be hung on the vast walls of the rotunda. Fiberglass was the answer. The first few steps in constructing a piece from fiberglass are the same as those of conventional sculpture: original sketches are reproduced in clay and a plaster mold is made.

378.

Welding leg sections together for *Christ on the Cross* at the foundry in Oslo, Norway, 1959

379.

Installation of *Christ on the Cross*, Cross in the Woods, Indian River, Michigan, 1959

From here the process differs. In the next step, the surface of the mold is coated with a light spray of releasing agent, and liquid plastic resin, the consistency of thick glue, is worked into the crevices. Thin fiberglass cloth is then spread over the interior surface of the mold and smoothed out. The fiberglass and resin are allowed to harden. This process is repeated three more times, permitting the form to harden between each application. When completely cured, the hardened form is removed from the mold, reproducing the original clay in exact detail. Each eight-foot-wide panel for the Ford Rotunda weighed only fifty pounds, but was nevertheless strong and stable, which made for more practical installation.

> To execute sculpture of monumental scale, the sculptor requires space, height, light, heat, equipment of all descriptions. Quantities of materials, assistants to help with the lifting, crating, enlarging, casting, and numerous other purely mechanical tasks that go into the creation of large-scale work. —MMF

To bring monumental architectural sculpture through all the different phases of development takes superhuman effort and attention to the smallest of details. Fredericks hired many skilled assistants over the years to help him on his commissions. Thomas Marker, Tosca Zagni, Oscar Graves, Herman Hogg, Pamela Stump, Molly Barth, and Scott Slocum were some of his more long-standing employees. After designing and building the artwork, the sculptor's role can be compared to that of the conductor of a great orchestra, directing, supervising, and in Fredericks's case often playing many of the instruments himself. All the functions necessary to the creation and installation of the work are carried out under the sculptor's guidance: excavation of the site, provision of water and electric facilities, engineering of the supporting concrete and steel, installation of pumping, spray systems, and lighting, and, finally, transportation and placement of the sculpture.

The final installation of a piece of monumental sculpture is a critical step and the manner in which it is attached to its base is

380.
Fredericks chasing an arm weld on the Christ figure for the
Indian River crucifix, 1959

given priority consideration. Civil engineers
are consulted and can advise as to weight
issues, the strength of prevailing winds,
atmospheric conditions, the tensile strength
of chosen materials. Generally, affixing
a piece of sculpture to its base is fairly
straightforward: heavy pins are welded to the
underside; a template is made, indicating the
location of the pins and these points are then
marked on the base. Holes are drilled to
accommodate the pins and then filled with
epoxy. The piece is lowered into place, the
pins slipping into the pre-drilled holes. This
process varies in complexity depending on
the peculiarities of the piece being installed.

The foundation and supportive steel
plates for the enormous redwood and bronze
Christ on the Cross at Indian River, Michigan
(fig. 238), had to be massively reinforced to
hold the weight of eighteen vertically oriented
tons. While Fredericks was working on the
twenty-eight-foot-high Christ figure in his
New York studio, redwood trees in California
were being inspected for size and density to
accommodate the fifty-five-foot-tall cross.
The clay work and plaster casting were done
in the studio and the finished plaster sections
were shipped to the foundry in Oslo to be
cast into bronze. There, the piece was cast in

sections, a temporary cross erected with
accompanying scaffolding, and the sections
lifted into vertical position so that they
could be accurately welded together. For
transporting back to the United States, the
bronze figure was cabled to the deck of a
ship, the arms left separate to be welded on
after the piece reached the Indian River site.
Once there, the arms were attached, welded
seams had to be chased, texture refigured,
and the patina reapplied. The wooden cross
having been put in place, an enormous system of scaffolding was erected around it to
facilitate the next step. The Christ figure
was lashed to a special steel platform that
was lifted up by cranes and bolted into position. The bolts themselves were thirty-two
inches in length.

The sixteen-foot-tall bronze figure for
The Spirit of Detroit (fig. 230) measures
twenty-three feet across, weighs nine tons,
and took four years to complete. The half-
scale clay model was built up in Fredericks's
New York studio, then the plaster was cast,
crated, and shipped to Oslo. The full-scale
enlargement of the piece required many trips
back and forth to oversee the work. When
completed, the sculpture, this time in one
piece, was wrapped in heavy layers of burlap
and affixed to a steel framework especially
built to protect it on its sea journey. Twelve
tons of sculpture and framework were lifted
into the hold of the German freighter
Thomas Schulte, the only ship large enough
to stow the statue below decks, yet small
enough to navigate the St. Lawrence Seaway.
When it arrived in Detroit, the sculpture was
lifted onto a heavy transport vehicle and,
with police escort, slowly driven through
the downtown area, special arrangements
having been made for the temporary removal
of power and phone lines along the route to
its location at the City-County Building.
Two cranes lowered the seated figure onto
its marble base, where steel dowels hold it
in place.

Fredericks worked on his most ambitious
project, the *Cleveland War Memorial* (fig. 289),
for nineteen years. Not only did he oversee
the work on the enormous bronze central

figure and the carving of the four flanking monolithic granite pieces, he also attended to the smallest details, such as the design of the 286 spray nozzles (in five different styles) that project the water in the granite basin in different configurations. He spent months perfecting the intricate lighting plan, which included floodlights within the filigreed sphere, and devising an enormous four-ton steel "mast" as part of a complex internal structure to hold the rising figure in its vertical position. He also worked out how to anchor the figure to the supporting flange that extended into the foundation below ground. For final shipment from the foundry in Oslo, the bronze figure was wrapped in protective cloth, encased in specially welded steel crating which held it securely, and not removed until the work was lifted into place at the site. The central figure's vertical thrust of forty-six feet, the bronze filigreed sphere at the base, and the granite reflecting pool were all planned to exist in perfect harmony with the buildings and city spaces surrounding the memorial. This, Fredericks's most momentous commission, took the joint efforts of scores of skilled professionals as well as countless Cleveland city officials to see the project to its completion.

A commission's journey from drafting table to dedication day can take years, a progression of many stages from concept to clay to plaster to finished material to final installation. Countless hours of mental and physical work are spent coordinating the infinite number of details involved in a single commission. Marshall Fredericks was a true master of all aspects of this often daunting work, and for sculptors now and in the future, his example will continue to educate and inspire.

Michaele Duffy Kramer

381.
Consulting with the architect on the *Cleveland War Memorial*, 1955

382.
The Spirit of Detroit en route to Detroit, 1958

Medallic Art as a Form of Sculpture:
A Selection of Fredericks's Minted Medallions

The technique of sculpture in relief, or a design projected from or sunk into a flat surface, is as old as the art of sculpture itself, but the medal as an independent art form first appeared in fifteenth-century Italy. Because the production process was difficult and lengthy most medals were unique objects or single issues, until the invention of the Janvier Machine in 1839 revolutionized the medium and made possible the issuance of multiple editions. The flowering of medallic art in America occurred primarily through the efforts of sculptor Augustus Saint-Gaudens (1848–1907), whose medals were much admired for their translation of the Beaux-Arts style into small scale. The revival he inspired was such that during the late nineteenth century, any sculptor of note incorporated medallic art into his body of work.

Medals had long been used as gifts and symbols of commemoration and honor, but by the early twentieth century they were increasingly viewed as collectible items. In the United States the popularity of medals was further increased by the formation of two series designed for collectors, the Circle of Friends of the Medallion in 1909 and the Society of Medalists in 1930. One of the important numismatic collectors in America was Archer Huntington, renowned arts patron and founder of Brookgreen Gardens. It is a particularly fitting acknowledgment of Marshall Fredericks's skill in this medium that in 1977 he was commissioned to create the Gardens' membership medal. In the special format of the art medal, Fredericks was able to clearly project his ideas, hopes, and dreams within the context of each medal's purpose.

Fredericks's unique blend of pure line and refined detail with his ability to capture the essence of the subject translated well from three-dimensional sculpture to the art of relief and the medal. His bold use of innovative shapes and materials coupled with unique interpretation of themes and subject matter created a number of interesting designs. The Craftsmanship Medal of the American Institute of Architects is a triangular shape and the Dow Chemical Corporation 50th Anniversary Medal was struck in gold-plated aluminum and magnesium. The Cranbrook Mary Soper Pope Memorial Award, designed in 1946, utilizes the dual themes of mother and child and teacher and student on the obverse. The reverse depicts nature in the form of plant life with a small lizard. For the 1962 American Numismatic Association Convention at Detroit he designed a medal featuring his landmark sculpture, *The Spirit of Detroit*, on the reverse. The left side of the obverse design, an American eagle, is mirrored on the right side by a grouping of maple leaves, signifying the first joint meeting of the American and the Canadian Numismatic Associations. His 1972 medal for Denmark's Rebild National Park Society features the American eagle and the official Danish coat of arms on the obverse, and Abraham Lincoln's profile and log cabin on the reverse.

Fredericks's design for the obverse of the Brookgreen Gardens Medal of 1977 features the image of his sculpture *Leaping Gazelle* from the Brookgreen collection. A nature scene with South Carolina's state bird, the Carolina wren, perched in rhododendron foliage is depicted on the reverse. The clean, low relief of the medal enhances a beautiful design offered in two patinas: polished bronze and torch green. Fredericks requested the latter to be struck in limited quantity for distribution to the Brookgreen Board of Trustees in order to distinguish the trustees' special medals from those distributed to members. The use of an unusual patina was one of many innovative ideas that he employed to enhance his medallic art designs. Fredericks's medal has been among the most popular of the long-running series for Brookgreen Gardens, now in its thirtieth year.

—Robin R. Salmon

383.

Michigan Horticultural Society

1941, minted in bronze, gold fill, and silver, diameter 3 inches, Michigan Horticultural Society, East Lansing, Michigan

Face: Bas-relief of sun and rain behind man planting a tree

Reverse: Inscription, "Michigan Horticultural Society," with bas-relief of potted topiary

Winner of medallic design contest for Annual Michigan Horticultural Society Exhibition.

384.

Lincoln National Life Insurance Company Medal

1942, minted in bronze, diameter 3 inches, Lincoln National Life Insurance Company, Indianapolis, Indiana (full-scale relief, bronze, diameter 24 inches)

Face: Inscription, "The Lincoln National Life Insurance Company," with bas-relief of Arthur F. Hall; in smaller type, "Company Founded 1905 Arthur F. Hall"

Reverse: Inscription, "He Held his Place—Held the Long Purpose—Like a Growing Tree"; in smaller type, "Quotation from Markham's Lincoln," with bas-relief of Abraham Lincoln sitting on a log, reading a book, hatchet by his side

385.

Mary Soper Pope Memorial Award

1946, minted in bronze, diameter 3 inches, Cranbrook Institute of Science, Bloomfield Hills, Michigan (full-scale relief, bronze, diameter 11 inches)

Face: Inscription, "Mary Soper Pope Memorial Award Cranbrook Institute of Science," with bas-relief of a kneeling woman teaching child about a seedling

Reverse: Bas-relief tulip design

Annual award created for exceptionally meritorious work in the plant sciences.

386.

Dow Chemical Corporation 50th Anniversary Medal

1947, minted in gold-plated aluminum and magnesium, diameter 3 inches, Dow Chemical Corporation, Midland, Michigan

Face: Inscription, "Fifty years of creative development 1897–1947," with bas-relief of hand holding a leaf towards the sun

Reverse: Planets swirling around the universe and Dow logo

Identified in 1983 catalogue for the Fédération Internationale de la Médaille (F.I.D.E.M.) as representative of medals produced for American industry.

387.

Eaton Manufacturing Medallion

1948, minted in bronze, diameter 3 inches, Eaton Manufacturing Company, Cleveland, Ohio. Based on the Eaton War Memorial Eagle (see fig. 123).

Face: Bas-relief of the Eaton War Memorial Eagle, signed "Marshall Fredericks"

Reverse: Inscription, "In honor of the men of this organization who gave their lives for their country," with bas-relief of laurel wreath

388.

Michigan Academy Award Medal

(prototype shown here), 1950, cast in bronze in the shape of an painter's palette, 2¹⁄₂ x 3¹⁄₂ inches, Michigan Academy of Science, Arts, and Letters, Ann Arbor, Michigan. Prototype in a private collection.

Face: Inscription, "Michigan Academy of Science Arts and Letters" with a bas-relief of a hand holding a female figure

Reverse: Inscriptions, "For outstanding contribution to the development of the arts in Michigan," and "Marshall M. Fredericks. Scp."; on the edge, the copyright symbol and "1950"; engraved in the center, "Presented to Marshall M. Fredericks"

Fredericks designed the medal for the Michigan Academy of Science, Arts, and Letters in 1950 and, in 1952, was the first person to receive the award (post-war), for his outstanding contribution to Michigan art.

389.

Michigan Society of Architects Medal

1954, minted in bronze and gold-plated bronze, 2 x 1⅝ inches, Michigan Society of Architects

Face: Inscription, "The Michigan Society of Architects," with bas-relief of society's shield

Reverse: Inscription, "A State Organization of the American Institute of Architects"

Award presented to a person chosen as having made the greatest contribution to the field of architecture in the past year.

390.

George and Ellen Booth Founders Medallion

1955, minted in bronze, diameter 3 inches, Cranbrook Educational Community, Bloomfield Hills, Michigan (full-scale relief, bronze, diameter 21 inches, George Gough Booth and Ellen Scripps Booth Memorial, Cranbrook Institute of Science, Bloomfield Hills, Michigan, 1950, see fig. 150)

Face: Inscription, "George Gough Booth—Ellen Scripps Booth," with their portrait reliefs

Reverse: Inscription, "Founders Medal—The Cranbrook Foundation"

Fredericks himself was the recipient of the 1991 Founders Medal, the highest award given by the Cranbrook Educational Community.

391.

American Institute of Architects Craftsmanship Medal

1960, minted in bronze and gold, 2¼–, 7–, and 11–inch triangles, American Institute of Architects, Washington, D.C. (shown in plaster)

Face: Inscription, "The American Institute of Architects," with bas-relief of male figure holding urn and looking upward

Created for a new category of awards established in 1960.

392.

Alexander Blain Senior and Alexander Blain, M.D., F.A.C.S.

1961, minted in bronze, rectangular plaquette, 3¼ x 2¹⁵⁄₁₆ and 1¼ x 1¹⁄₁₆ inches, Blain Hospital, Detroit, Michigan (full-scale relief, bronze, 36½ x 31 inches)

Face: Inscription, "Alexander Blain Senior 1840–1932 Alexander Blain M.D.F.A.C.S 1885–1958," with bas-relief portraits of father and son.

393.

American-Canadian Numismatic Association

1962, minted in bronze, gold, and silver, diameter 1⁵⁄₈ inches, American and Canadian Joint Numismatic Association Convention, Detroit, Michigan.

Face: Inscription, "American Canadian Numismatic Associations," with bas-relief of the official symbols of both countries, an American eagle and maple leaves, split in half to reflect the cooperation of both countries

Reverse: Inscription, "Annual Convention Detroit, Michigan 1962," with bas-relief of *The Spirit of Detroit* (see fig. 230)

The medal was created for the first annual joint convention of the Numismatic Associations of Canada and the United States.

394.

Detroit Mayor's Medal

1963, minted in bronze, gold fill, and gold-plated bronze, diameter 1½ and 2½ inches, City of Detroit, Michigan

Face: Inscription "The Spirit of Detroit" above bas-relief of *The Spirit of Detroit* (see fig. 230) with "Presented by Mayor Jerome P. Cavanagh" below

Reverse: Inscription, "The City of Detroit" above the seal of the city of Detroit with "Michigan" below, "Speramus Meliora" to the left and "Resurget Cineribus" to the right.

Medals presented by the Mayor of Detroit include the Medal of Distinction, presented in a leather box, and the Distinguished Service Medal.

395.

Tracy W. McGregor

1964, rectangular plaquette, minted in bronze, 3¼ x 2¾ inches, Tracy W. McGregor Library of American History, University of Virginia, Charlottesville, Virginia (full-scale relief, bronze, 36½ x 31½ inches) (shown in plaster)

Face: Inscription, "Tracy W. McGregor, Philanthropist, Humanitarian, Educator, 1869–1936," with portrait relief

396.

Jefferson National Expansion Memorial Medallion

1965, minted in bronze and silver, diameter 2½ and 1½ inches, issued by the National Park Service and the Jefferson National Expansion Memorial Association in connection with Eero Saarinen and Associates

Face: Inscription, "Jefferson National Expansion Memorial St. Louis Missouri," with bas-relief male figure

Reverse: Inscription, "Gateway to the West," with bas-relief of St. Louis Arch, courthouse, and skyline

397.

Oakland County Sesqui-Centennial Coin

1970, minted in bronze and silver, diameter 1½ inches, Oakland County, Michigan

Face: Inscription, "County of Oakland Michigan," with bas-relief of sunburst behind white-oak tree

Reverse: Inscription, "Sesqui-Centennial 1820–1970," with bas-relief of Chief Pontiac carrying a peace pipe, representing the dream of all men, behind his head a full moon, signifying the end of an era

Commemorative coin sold only in banks and financial institutions during Oakland County's Sesqui-Centennial.

398.

Rebild American Independence Day Medal

1972, minted in gold, silver, and bronze, diameter 1¼ and 3 inches, Rebild National Park Society, Jutland, Denmark

Face: Inscription, "Tilegnet Den Danske Og Amerikanske Befolkning Til Evigt Venskab (Dedicated to the Eternal Friendship of the Danish and American People)," with bas-relief design of American eagle overlapping the Danish coat of arms

Reverse: Inscription, "Rebild National Park Society, Inc. Commemorating American Independence Day," with bas-reliefs of President Lincoln and his log cabin birthplace

The Rebild National Park was purchased by Danish-born Americans to be a site for annual reunions and was deeded to the Danish government in 1912. The medal was produced to recognize the friendship between both countries and as a source of revenue.

399.

Henry Ford Medallion

1975, minted in bronze, diameter 1½ inches, Manufacturers Bank, Dearborn, Michigan.

Face: Inscription, "Henry Ford Memorial Dearborn, Michigan," with bas-relief of Henry Ford in a characteristic pose with hands in his pockets

Reverse: Inscription, "Education is the greatest force of civilization, quotation on Henry Ford Memorial," with bas-reliefs of architectural landmarks of Dearborn and symbols of transportation

Produced as a memento of the dedication of the memorial in front of the Henry Ford Centennial Library (see fig. 315)

400.

The Gazelle Medal (Brookgreen Gardens Membership Medal)

1977, minted in bronze, diameter 3 inches, Brookgreen Gardens, Pawleys Island, South Carolina. Based on *Leaping Gazelle* in the collection of Brookgreen Gardens

Face: Inscription, "Brookgreen Gardens, South Carolina," with bas-relief of *Leaping Gazelle*

Reverse: Two wrens, South Carolina's state bird, perched on rhododendrons

Presented to Sustaining, Patron, and Life members in 1977; also part of Brookgreen Gardens Annual Medallic Series. Exhibited as United States entry at the Biennial Exhibition of the Féderation Internationale de la Médaille (F.I.D.E.M) in Florence, Italy, 1983.

401.

Charles F. Kettering Medal, Charles S. Mott Medal, and Alfred P. Sloan Medal

1979, minted in bronze and gold-plated bronze, diameter 2¼ inch (each), General Motors Cancer Research Foundation, Detroit, Michigan (shown in plaster)

Face: Portrait relief of named individual

Reverse: Inscription, "General Motors Cancer Research Foundation"

The awards recognize basic and clinical scientists throughout the world who have been selected by their peers for demonstrated achievements in research directed at the discovery of the cause, prevention, and treatment of cancer.

402.

American Numismatic Association 93rd Anniversary Convention

1984, minted in bronze, diameter 1¹/₄ inches and 2¹/₄ inches, American Numismatic Association, Detroit, Michigan

(shown in plaster)

Face: Abstract eagle representing a blend of the *Victory Eagle* designed for the Veterans Memorial Building in Detroit (see fig. 135) and the *American Eagle* on Cincinnati's Federal Building (see fig. 265)

Reverse: Inscription, "American Numismatic Association 93rd Anniversary Convention, Detroit, Michigan 1984," with bas-relief of book and oil lamp

403.

Flying Wild Geese Medallion

1988, minted in bronze, diameter 2³/₄ inches, Marshall M. Fredericks Sculpture Museum, Saginaw Valley State University, University Center, Michigan. Based on *Flying Wild Geese*, 1955 (see fig. 207).

Face: Flying wild geese in bas-relief encircled by stars

Reverse: Inscription, "Arbury Fine Arts Center Marshall M. Fredericks Sculpture Gallery, Saginaw Valley State University 1963," with triangular bas-relief of the university's insignia

Boxed with an easel for display, in a limited edition of 400 to benefit the Marshall M. Fredericks Sculpture Museum.

404.
From left: Fredericks's father Frank,
Fredericks, his sister Margaret, mother
Frances, brothers Frank and James

1908

Born Marshall Maynard Fredericks, the youngest of four children, on January 31, to Frank Arthur Fredericks and Frances Margaret Bragg, in the Scandinavian community of Rock Island, Illinois. Paternal grandparents, Matt Frederiksen and Anna Christensen, had emigrated there from Denmark and Norway in the 1860s.

1912

Claims to have carved his first sculpture from a bar of laundry soap at the age of four, igniting a lifelong interest in artistic expression.

1915

Family moves to Florida so Fredericks's father can pursue engineering projects.

1917

Family moves again, to Cleveland, Ohio.

As a teen, works with his father, a construction engineer, learning technical and mechanical skills.

1924

Attends John Huntington Polytechnic Institute in Cleveland, prior to enrolling for four years at the Cleveland School of Art (now the Cleveland Institute of Art).

1930

Graduates from the Cleveland School of Art and is awarded the Herman Matzen Traveling Scholarship in Sculpture.

Travels to Scandinavia, meets sculptor Carl Milles, and works in his carving shop, learning to carve marble and granite. For several months, he continues his studies and travels through Europe, taking courses in Germany at the Kunstakademie, working at the Heimann Schule, and learning armature and casting techniques from sculptor Hans Schwegerle. In Paris studies at the Académie Scandinav, then travels through Italy, Spain, and North Africa, returning to Germany to complete some projects.

1931

Returns to the United States and becomes part-time instructor in sculpture at the Cleveland School of Art while working on and exhibiting his own work.

1932

Invited by Carl Milles to assist in his studio at the Cranbrook Academy of Art in Bloomfield Hills, Michigan.

1933

Receives scholarship for study with Carl Milles at the Cranbrook Academy of Art. Appointed to teach sculpture, wood carving, and ceramics at Kingswood School and to teach art at Cranbrook School. Continues working with Milles and gains experience creating monumental sculptures and refining the mechanics of engineering large works.

1934

Appointed instructor of ceramics and modeling at the Cranbrook Academy of Art (through 1938).

1936

Wins national award competition to design a fountain for the Levi L. Barbour Memorial, located on Belle Isle, an island park belonging to the city of Detroit.

1938

Based on his receiving honorable mention for sketch models submitted to 1939 New York World's Fair United States Government Building Competition, the Treasury Department's Section of Painting and Sculpture invites and accepts his designs for post offices in River Rouge, Michigan, and Sandwich, Illinois.

Teaches in the sculpture department at the Cranbrook Academy of Art (until his departure in 1942).

1939

Baboon Fountain installed for Glass Industries Building at the New York World's Fair. It is selected by the city of New York's Department of Parks as one of six sculptures from the exposition worthy of permanent location after the close of the fair. Unfortunately, the temporary stone castings are destroyed during the war and the intended granite fountain is never reproduced.

Selected by Malcolm R. Stirton, chief designer for the architectural firm of Harley, Ellington and Day, to collaborate on the design of the Horace H. Rackham Educational Memorial Building in Detroit.

405.
Milles and Fredericks in sculpture
class at Kingswood School,
Cranbrook

406.
New Yorker cartoon depicting
one of Fredericks's baboons at the
1939 New York World's Fair

1942

Volunteers for the armed forces. Assigned to the
Army Corps of Engineers in Arizona, he reacquaints
himself with a volunteer driver on the base, Rosalind
Bell Cooke, whom he had met earlier in Michigan.

Horace H. Rackham Memorial Educational Building
is dedicated.

1943

Marries Rosalind Bell Cooke on September 9, 1943,
and is transferred to the Eighth Army Air Corps.

1944

Twin sons, Christopher and Carl, born May 13. (Carl
is named in honor of Fredericks's mentor, Carl Milles.)

Serves with the Intelligence Section of the Twentieth
Bombing Squad in the India-Burma Theatre (India,
China, the Philippines, and Okinawa).

1945

Awarded rank of lieutenant colonel prior to discharge.

Returns to Michigan and establishes a studio in
Royal Oak.

Immediately upon return to civilian life is selected to
design a World War II memorial for Cleveland, Ohio.

1946

Daughter Frances born June 20.

1948

Completes *Spirit of Kentucky*, free-form reliefs for
the Courier-Journal Building in Louisville, Kentucky.

1949

Collaborates again with the architectural firm of
Harley, Ellington and Day on the Administration
Building (now the Literature, Science and Arts
Building) at the University of Michigan in Ann Arbor.

Chairs the Fine Arts Section of the Michigan
Academy of Science, Arts, and Letters.

Anchors a television series, "The World of Art," pro-
duced by Chrysler Motors in cooperation with the
Detroit Institute of Arts, for WXYZ-TV, Channel 7,
Detroit.

Daughter Rosalind born March 30.

1950

Establishes working studios in New York City and
in Norway to accommodate the monumental bronze
castings required to complete the Cleveland War
Memorial commission and to gain access to
Norwegian granite carvers. Introduces and exports
Norwegian granites to the United States.

Installs carved marble *Victory Eagle* on façade of the
Veterans Memorial Building (now the UAW-Ford
National Program Center) in Detroit, another building designed by Harley, Ellington and Day, drawing
the attention of the Michigan Society of Architects.

1951

Completes award-winning limestone reliefs for the
Ohio Union Building at Ohio State University in
Columbus.

1952

Receives the coveted Fine Arts Medal from the
American Institute of Architects.

Asked to create a monumental crucifix for a chapel
at Indian River in northern Michigan.

1953

Daughter Suzanne born May 21.

The Ford Rotunda in Dearborn is remodeled.
Fredericks casts sixteen reliefs in fiberglass polyester
resin laminate for the interior, and Buckminster
Fuller designs a geodesic dome for the roof. The
Rotunda becomes the fifth most-visited tourist site
in the country.

Works with car companies, designing hood ornaments
for Chrysler Motors, General Motors Corporation,
and Studebaker-Packard Corporation.

407.
Major Fredericks during the time he was stationed in India, 1944–45

408.
Fredericks's studio on Woodward Avenue in Royal Oak, Michigan

1954

Designs stainless steel and fiberglass furniture for the Holden Great Ape House at the Detroit Zoo.

Carves *The Boy and Bear* for Northland Shopping Center in Southfield, Michigan. Designed by Victor Gruen, Northland is one of the world's first shopping centers.

1955

Carl Milles dies.

Fredericks expands his use of fiberglass, creating bas-reliefs of the 1955 Chevrolet for ten billboards across the United States.

1956

Continuing his experimentation with various media, creates *The Ford Empire*, a 145-foot-long span of aluminum and brass for the Henry and Edsel Ford Auditorium in Detroit.

1957

Carves the *The Lion and Mouse* for Eastland Shopping Center in Harper Woods, Michigan, another early shopping center designed by Victor Gruen.

1958

Dedication of the *Memorial to Norwegian Emigrants* (a full-scale casting of *Leaping Gazelle*) in Stavanger, Norway. Fredericks donated the sculpture as a symbol of friendship between the United States and Norway and presented it to King Olav V. The work commemorates the men and women of Norwegian blood who have contributed to the building of America.

The Spirit of Detroit (commissioned in 1955) is shipped from the foundry in Oslo, Norway, and installed in front of Harley, Ellington and Day's new City-County Building (now the Coleman A. Young Municipal Center) in Detroit.

1959

Dedication of *Christ on the Cross*, believed to be the largest crucifix in the world, in Indian River, Michigan, August 16.

1960

Opens the "Greenhouse" and the "Stable" in Bloomfield Hills, Michigan, as extensions of his Royal Oak studio.

On two different state occasions, presents small-scale models of *The Spirit of Detroit* to the President of Finland, Dr. Urho K. Kekkonen, and to President Dwight D. Eisenhower.

1964

The Expanding Universe fountain (commissioned in 1956 by the General Services Administration) is installed and dedicated at the State Department Building, Washington, D.C.

President Lyndon Johnson receives a small-scale model of *The Spirit of Detroit*.

Freedom of the Human Spirit (commissioned by the city of New York in 1960) is installed at the 1964 New York World's Fair.

The *Cleveland War Memorial: Fountain of Eternal Life* (which had required nineteen years to complete) is dedicated on Memorial Day, May 30.

1965

Presents Prince Bernhard of the Netherlands with a small-scale model of *The Spirit of Detroit*.

In cooperation with the Lord Mayor of Copenhagen, Urban Hansen, and with the patronage of Princess Benedikte of Denmark, establishes DIADEM (Disabled Americans' Denmark Meeting), an exchange program between Denmark and the United States for disabled young adults.

409.
The artist with his family, from left: Fran, Roz, Carl, wife Roz with Suki, and Chris. c. 1953

410.
Working on the billboard for the 1955 Chevrolet

Beginning in December, serves as acting Danish Consul for the state of Michigan.

Princess Benedikte receives a small-scale model of *The Spirit of Detroit*.

1967
Co-chairs DIADEM Return, a reciprocal visit jointly sponsored by the Easter Seal Society and by the Committee for the Handicapped of the People-to-People Program, bringing an exchange group of fifty disabled young Danish adults to the United States.

Detroit Mayor Jerome P. Cavanagh declares July 14 DIADEM Day.

1968
On May 18 is appointed by Danish King Frederik IX as Royal Danish Consul for the state of Michigan, a position he retains for thirty years.

1969
Co-Chairs DIADEM Leader, which enrolls Danish students and trainers at the Leader Dogs for the Blind School in Rochester, Michigan; sends fourteen leader dogs back to Denmark, with hopes of launching a similar program there.

1971
Detroit Mayor Roman S. Gribbs presents President Richard M. Nixon with a small-scale model of *The Spirit of Detroit*.

Fredericks is one of the founding members of Michigan Artrain (now Artrain USA)—the nation's only traveling art museum on a train; remains involved as a board member for many years.

1973
Second DIADEM Leader project at Leader Dogs for the Blind.

1974
Elected to the Board of Trustees of Brookgreen Gardens, Pawleys Island, South Carolina, a position he holds until his death, serving at various times as chairman of the Art Committee as well as on the Fundraising and Design and Review Committees.

1975
Appointed by Michigan Governor William G. Milliken to serve on the Special Commission on Art in State Buildings.

Invited to be the American speaker for the annual July 4 Celebration at Rebild National Park in Aalborg, Denmark.

1977
Designs the Brookgreen Gardens Membership Medal for the Brookgreen Gardens medal series—the only medallic series known to be issued by a museum.

1980
Donates small-scale casting of *Freedom of the Human Spirit* to serve as the annual Communications Award of the International Center for the Disabled (ICD), an organization of which he is a longtime benefactor. The award is the highest honor bestowed by the ICD.

1981
DIADEM Leader Return brings another group of blind students from Denmark to train with Leader Dogs for the Blind.

The International Center for the Disabled honors Danish Queen Benedikte at the annual ICD Dinner, recognizing her support of DIADEM.

1983
Detroit Mayor Coleman A. Young presents Mayor Nishiyama of Toyota City, Japan, with a model of

411.
Norwegian King Olav V at the dedication of the Memorial to Norwegian Emigrants in Stavanger, Norway, in 1958

The Spirit of Detroit, which is intended for permanent display in Detroit's sister city.

Birmingham, Michigan, commissions a full-scale casting of *Freedom of the Human Spirit* in honor of the city's fiftieth anniversary. The sculpture is installed in Shain Park and dedicated in 1988.

1984
Receives the Michigan Academy Award from the Michigan Academy of Science, Arts, and Letters.

1985
Birmingham City Commissioner Geoffrey Hockman presents a small-scale model of *Freedom of the Human Spirit* to Mayor Ikai and the city fathers of Ritto, Japan, Birmingham's sister city.

1986
Don Peterson, chairman of Ford Motor Company and a personal friend as well as staunch advocate of Fredericks, is honored with Brookgreen Gardens's first American Achievement Award (a model of *Leaping Gazelle*).

Fredericks is accorded the rare honor of being asked to sign one of the ceiling beams at Detroit's Scarab Club, an organization of artists founded in 1910.

Groundbreaking for the Arbury Fine Arts Center at Saginaw Valley State University in University

412.
Detroit Mayor Jerome P. Cavanagh and Fredericks present President Lyndon Johnson with *The Spirit of Detroit*, 1964

Center, Michigan. The Fine Arts Center will eventually include the Marshall M. Fredericks Sculpture Gallery.

1988
Appointed to the Artistic Advisory Board of the Interlochen Center for the Arts, Interlochen, Michigan.

Dedication of the Marshall M. Fredericks Sculpture Gallery (the name will later be changed to the Marshall M. Fredericks Sculpture Museum) at Saginaw Valley State University, May 15.

Named chairman of the Art Committee at Brookgreen Gardens.

1989
Participates at the Cleveland Preservation Symposium IV in response to a controversy surrounding the approval of a parking garage under the Cleveland War Memorial fountain.

1992
Conservation of the *Fountain of Eternal Life*.

1993
The United States Ambassador to Canada, James Blanchard, invites Fredericks to participate in the Art in Embassies program, "communicating American values and cultural diversity through the display of American art at overseas posts."

1994
Presents Detroit Mayor Dennis Archer with a model of *The Spirit of Detroit*. Archer becomes the last of a select few, including only two other mayors, six heads of state, and five presidents to receive a small-scale model of *The Spirit*.

Dedication of *Nordic Swan and the Ugly Duckling* at the Danish Embassy in Washington, D.C.

413.
DIADEM Return participants arriving in
the United States from Denmark, 1967

414.
Fredericks receives honorary doctorate at
Dana College in Blair, Nebraska, 1980

Northland Center commissions Detroit's Pewabic
Pottery to produce limited edition tiles depicting *The
Boy and Bear* to commemorate the shopping center's
fortieth anniversary.

1995

Birmingham Community Education and the
Beaumont Foundation sponsor a community-wide
"Photo Safari," the aim of which is to locate
Fredericks's works in the community.

More than two dozen of his sculptures, including
two previously uncast versions of the *The Friendly
Dragon*, are displayed in the newly opened Frederik
Meijer Gardens and Sculpture Park in Grand Rapids,
Michigan.

Enlarges a 1930s sketch model by Carl Milles into
an eighty-six-foot-high bronze sculpture, *God and
the Rainbow*. Travels to Sweden to dedicate its
placement over the Nacka Strand, across the fjord
from Millesgården.

1996

The Expanding Universe fountain undergoes a complete conservation treatment and is rededicated.

Freedom of the Human Spirit conserved and rein-
stalled at its permanent site as part of Flushing
Meadow-Corona Park in New York.

Torso of a Dancer selected for exhibition in the permanent collection of the Smithsonian American Art
Museum, Washington, D.C.

1997

At age eighty-nine, Fredericks completes the *Star
Dream Fountain*, which is installed and dedicated at
the Barbara Hallman Plaza, Royal Oak, Michigan.

Birth of the Atomic Age (originally installed in 1959)
is conserved and rededicated at the National
Exchange Club in Toledo, Ohio.

The Spirit of Detroit is outfitted in a Red Wings jersey
in celebration of the Detroit hockey team's winning
the Stanley Cup.

1998

Completes full-scale clay model of last monumental
work, *Lord Byron*.

Attends ninetieth birthday celebration at the
Birmingham Community House, attended by family
and local and international friends.

Marshall Maynard Fredericks works at his Royal Oak
Studio until three days before his death on April 4.

Premier performance of Catherine McMichael's
choral work "The Saints and Sinners," inspired by
Fredericks's work of the same name, on May 16, at
Saginaw Valley State University, in celebration of the
tenth anniversary of the Marshall M. Fredericks
Sculpture Museum and Fredericks's ninetieth birthday.

415.
A last laugh in honor of Fredericks (cartoon by
Bill Day, *Detroit Free Press*, April 5, 1998)

Achievements and Honors

1928

Awarded the Virginia Kelley Newberry Scholarship for the academic year 1928–1929, Cleveland School of Art.

1929

Awarded part of the Mrs. Lyman H. Treadway Scholarship for the academic year 1929–1930, Cleveland School of Art.

1930

Awarded the $1,000 Herman Matzen Traveling Scholarship in Sculpture upon graduation from the Cleveland School of Art.

1945

Awarded six Bronze Stars for meritorious service (as a major in the Army Air Corps), including a merit citation for his development of a new type of map for radar operators and a new method of simulating the probable appearance of the radarscope when flying over new territory. Promoted to the rank of lieutenant colonel prior to discharge.

1952

Awarded the American Institute of Architects Fine Arts Medal, a distinction awarded only five times between 1914 and 1998.

Presented with the Michigan Academy Award, for his outstanding contribution to the development of the arts in Michigan, by the Michigan Academy of Science, Arts, and Letters.

1953

First sculptor to be given honorary life membership in the Michigan Society of Architects.

1955

Reliefs for the Ohio Union at Ohio State University garner an Honorable Mention from the Architectural League of New York.

1956

The Architectural League of New York awards Fredericks its Gold Medal in Sculpture for the bas-reliefs at the Ford Rotunda in Dearborn, Michigan, and at Beaumont Hospital in Royal Oak, Michigan.

1957

Declared an Associate of the National Academy of Design, entitled to wear the Associate's Ribbon.

Elected a member of the National Sculpture Society.

1959

Given an honorary membership in the National Society of Interior Designers.

Elected a Life Fellow by the International Institute of Arts and Letters.

Mayor Louis C. Miriani presents the key to the city of Detroit to Mr. and Mrs. Marshall Fredericks on their sixteenth wedding anniversary.

1961

Becomes a Fellow of the National Sculpture Society.

Named a National Academician by the National Academy of Design.

1963

King Frederik IX of Denmark bestows upon Fredericks the Knighthood of the Order of Dannebrog.

Receives a Certificate of Merit from the National Academy of Design.

1964

Recognized by Governor and Mrs. George Romney at a reception honoring Michigan artists.

1965

Receives Michigan State Medical Society Centennial Award.

1967

Receives the Distinguished Award of the Year from the Michigan Association of Professions, recognizing him as the MAP member who best represented his profession during the preceding year.

The People-to-People Committee for the Handicapped awards Fredericks a Citation for Outstanding Contribution to International Goodwill, in recognition of his work with DIADEM and DIADEM Return

1968

Honored with the Golden Plate Award by the American Academy of Achievement.

1969

Receives a Certificate of Award from the Oakland County Association for Retarded Children.

Elected a Fellow of the Royal Society for the Encouragement of Arts, Manufactures and Commerce, London.

1971

Elevated as a Knight of the Order of Dannebrog, First Degree, by King Frederik IX of Denmark.

Receives the Wisdom Award of Honor from the Wisdom Society, for his role in the advancement of knowledge, learning, and research in education.

1972

Proclaimed *Borgmester for En Dag* (Mayor for the Day) by the Dansk-Amerikansk Klub, Aalborg, Denmark, and given the key to the city on July 4.

King Olav V of Norway confers upon Fredericks the Knighthood of the Royal Norwegian Order of St. Olav, First Class, Norway's highest civilian decoration.

Awarded the Henry Hering Memorial Medal by the National Sculpture Society for the Ohio Union reliefs.

Presented with the key to the city by Detroit Mayor Roman S. Gribbs, who proclaims August 18 to be Marshall M. Fredericks Day.

1973

Receives the President's Cabinet Medallion from the University of Detroit.

Elected a Fellow of the International Consular Academy.

1975

Michigan Governor William G. Milliken appoints Fredericks a member of the Special Commission on Art in State Buildings.

1978

Appointed a Commander of the Order of Dannebrog by Queen Margrethe II of Denmark and receives the Commander's Cross.

1979

Receives Michigan International Council Award.

Presented with the Portuguese Red Cross of Merit, the highest distinction awarded by the Red Cross.

1980

Receives honorary Doctor of Fine Arts degree from Dana College in Blair, Nebraska.

Receives honorary Doctor of Fine Arts degree from Saginaw Valley State College in Michigan (now Saginaw Valley State University).

Presented with the Commander's Cross of Poland's Rebirth, in honor of services rendered in the cause of a free Poland, and the Golden Cross of Merit, for achievements in the field of art and culture, by the president of the Polish Republic.

1982

Receives an "Honor Diploma" from the Belgian High Fidelity and Technology Institute for high merit in promoting sculpture and fine arts.

Awarded the Herbert Adams Memorial Medal for outstanding achievement in American sculpture by the National Sculpture Society.

Given a Special Tribute from the state of Michigan by Governor William G. Milliken and State Representative Ruth B. McNamee.

Awarded the Medal of Honor by the minister of culture of the Netherlands.

1983

On his seventy-fifth birthday, Fredericks receives congratulations from President Ronald Reagan and Governor William G. Milliken. He is honored by Michigan House Concurrent Resolution No. 244, in recognition of and gratitude for his many contributions to the enrichment of human life.

Named a Michigan Minuteman, concurrent with the state's celebration of Michigan Week.

The city of Birmingham, Michigan, proclaims May 16 to be Marshall M. Fredericks Day and awards Fredericks the key to the city.

Named an International Advisor to the International Center for the Disabled (ICD).

1984

Awarded the Michigan Academy of Science, Arts, and Letters Medal for Creative Achievement in the Arts.

1985

Receives an Award of Honor, in recognition of his service in the Armed Forces, from Bloomfield Hills, Michigan.

Fredericks is the subject of a Proclamation of Appreciation signed by Robert E. Hewitt, mayor of Greenville, Michigan.

Given an honorary membership in the Scarab Club of Detroit.

Receives the Special Medal of Honor for Notable Achievement in American Sculpture, the National Sculpture Society's highest award.

Awarded the *Médaille du rayonnement culturelle* and *La Médaille d'or au litres des artes plastiques* by the French government.

1986

Subject of a Detroit City Council Resolution citing his outstanding contributions to the world of art.

Recognized by Michigan Senate Resolution No. 385, on the occasion of his being honored by the American Scandinavian Foundation at the Michigan Associates Ball.

The International Institute of Detroit inducts Fredericks into its International Heritage Hall of Fame.

Birmingham Mayor Gary Kain presents Fredericks with a Freedom of the Human Spirit Resolution and a key to the city at the dedication of *Freedom of the Human Spirit* on September 7. Fredericks also receives a tribute from Michigan Governor James J. Blanchard.

Declared the first honorary member of the American Society of Landscape Architects, Michigan Chapter, and given an award of special recognition for outstanding contributions to the visual environment.

1987

Named a Knight of Grace by the Office of the Inspector General of the Americas, Organization of American States.

1988

Named Michigan Artist of the Year by Michigan Artrain.

Recognized by Michigan House Concurrent Resolution No. 770, in tribute to and recognition of his numerous contributions to artistic education.

1989

Honored with "A Tribute to Marshall Fredericks" at the Silver Celebration of the Danish Festival in Greenville, Michigan.

Commended by the city of Southfield, Michigan, for commitment to the city and its cultural arts endeavors.

Presented with the key to the city of Royal Oak, Michigan, by Mayor Robert Stocker.

Presented with an Appreciation Plaque by the Twenty-Second Regional Meeting of the American Chemical Society.

Named Honorary Chairman of the Center for Creative Studies-College of Art and Design's Alumni Fine Art Invitational, "Vernissage," held in conjunction with Preston-Burke Galleries.

1991

Receives the Cranbrook Educational Community's highest honor, the Founders Award.

Commended by Detroit Mayor Coleman A. Young on Senior Citizens' Day.

1992

Given an honorary membership in Denmark's Rebild National Park Society.

The American-Scandinavian Foundation of New York presents Fredericks with its prestigious Silver Medal Arts Award for service to America and Scandinavia.

1993

Awarded the International Achievement Award, one of the Governor's Arts Awards, by the Concerned Citizens for the Arts in Michigan; this is an honor given to a Michiganian who has achieved international prominence in the arts.

Receives a citation for distinguished service from the Michigan State Senate.

Awarded the Ellis Island Medal of Honor by the National Ethnic Coalition of Organizations in appreciation of his work as a humanitarian, sculptor, and Royal Danish Consul for Michigan. His receipt of the medal is entered into the Congressional Record of the 103rd Congress on July 13.

1994

Cleveland Mayor Michael R. White proclaims January 31 to be Marshall M. Fredericks Day.

1995

Named an honorary member of the National Honor Society by Birmingham Seaholm High School.

Knighted by King Carl XVI Gustaf of Sweden, receiving the Commander's Cross of the Royal Order of the Polar Star.

Granted the rank of Knight Grand Commander by the international Order of the Noble Companions of the Swan.

Honored by the United States Immigration and Naturalization Service, Detroit District, with an Award of Appreciation for his service as Royal Danish Consul.

1996

Receives the All-Area Arts Award in recognition of his contributions to the arts in Saginaw, Michigan, from the Saginaw Community Enrichment Commission.

Detroit Mayor Dennis Archer proclaims January 31 to be Marshall Fredericks Day in honor of Fredericks's eighty-eighth birthday and recognizes Fredericks's sculpture for being the "symbol of the spirit of the City of Detroit."

Honored with a special award by the International Center for the Disabled, New York, for his work with the disabled.

Recognized by President Bill Clinton, Vice President Al Gore, Secretary of State Warren Christopher, and Program Chairman Patrick Kennedy for his contributions to the United States Department of State's Art in Embassies program.

1997

Presented with a Lifetime Achievement Award by the Cultural Council of Birmingham/Bloomfield.

Receives the American Achievement Award from Brookgreen Gardens; this award has been granted only four times.

Named one of Brookgreen Gardens initial life trustees.

Michigan Senate Resolution No. 42 commemorates the work of Marshall M. Fredericks.

1998

Recognized by the Very Special Arts Michigan program for his invaluable support in providing access and opportunities for children and adults with disabilities to grow through the arts.

On the occasion of his ninetieth birthday celebration at the Community House in Birmingham Michigan, proclamations honoring Fredericks are offered by King Carl XVI Gustaf of Sweden, Queen Margrethe II of Denmark, Mayor Michael R. White of Cleveland, Ohio, Michigan State Senator Michael Bouchard, and other community leaders and dignitaries.

Cleveland Mayor Michael R. White signs a city proclamation in loving memory of Marshall M. Fredericks.

Resolution No. 166, memorializing "the life and work of sculptor Marshall Fredericks" is adopted by the Michigan Senate on April 14.

Exhibitions

Exhibited Sculptures, Catalogues, and Related Awards

1928

"Cleveland Museum of Art Tenth Annual Exhibition," April 25–June 3. Catalogue: *Bulletin of the Cleveland Museum of Art*, foreword by W. M. Milliken.

1929

"Cleveland Museum of Art Eleventh Annual Exhibition," April 23–June 2. Catalogue: *Bulletin of the Cleveland Museum of Art*, foreword by W. M. Milliken.

1930

"Cleveland Museum of Art Twelfth Annual Exhibition," April 22–June 1. Catalogue: *Bulletin of the Cleveland Museum of Art*, foreword by W. M. Milliken (*Figure Composition*).

1931

"First Annual Exhibit," Cleveland Sculptor's Club, Webb C. Ball Galleries, Cleveland (*Portrait of a Japanese, Portrait of Russell Aitken, Figure Composition*).

"Thirteenth Annual Exhibition," Cleveland Museum of Art, May 6–June 7. Catalogue: *Bulletin of the Cleveland Museum of Art*, foreword by W. M. Milliken (*Portrait of a Japanese*: First Prize, Sculpture—Models or Finished Work).

1932

"One Hundred Twenty-Seventh Annual Exhibition," Pennsylvania Academy of the Fine Arts, January 24–March 13 (*Portrait of a Japanese*).

"Fourteenth Annual Exhibition of Work by Cleveland Artists and Craftsmen," Cleveland Museum of Art, April 27–June 5. Catalogue: *Bulletin of the Cleveland Museum of Art*, foreword by W. M. Milliken (*Portrait of Dr. Henry John*: Certificate of Merit of the Third Class).

"Exhibition of Sculpture by Marshall Fredericks," Potter-Bentley Studios, Cleveland, October 24–November 5. Solo Exhibition.

Exhibition, Art Department, Ohio State Fair (*Chinese Girl*).

1933

"One Hundred Twenty-Eighth Annual Exhibition," Pennsylvania Academy of the Fine Arts, Philadelphia, January 29–March 19 (*Old Negro, Chinese Girl*).

1936

"Forty-Seventh Annual Exhibition of American Paintings and Sculpture," Art Institute of Chicago, October 21–December 6. Catalogue (*Bacchante*).

"One Hundred Thirty-First Annual Exhibition," Pennsylvania Academy of the Fine Arts, Philadelphia, January 26–March 1 (*Bacchante*).

1937

"Dance International 1900–1937, Exhibit of Arts Relating to the Dance," Rockefeller Center, New York. Catalogue, foreword by Mary Fanton Roberts (*Dancing Bacchante [Persephone]*: First Prize).

1938

Exhibition, Arden Gallery, New York, October 12–November 5 (*Acrobat, Juggler, and Lovesick Clowns*).

"First National Exhibition, Fifty-Second Annual Exhibition," Architectural League, New York. Catalogue (model of *Levi L. Barbour Memorial Fountain*).

"Forty-Ninth Annual Exhibition of American Paintings and Sculpture," Art Institute of Chicago, October 20–December 4. Catalogue (*Sisters [Two Sisters]*).

"Annual Exhibition for Michigan Artists," Detroit Institute of Arts, November 15–December 18. Catalogue, foreword by Clyde H. Burroughs (*Torso of a Dancer*: Anna Scripps Whitcomb Prize; *Two Sisters*).

1939

"Annual Exhibition for Michigan Artists," Detroit Institute of Arts, December 15–January 14, 1940. Catalogue, foreword by Clyde H. Burroughs (*Acrobat, Juggler, and Heartsick Clowns; Portrait of a Japanese*).

"Annual Faculty Exhibition," Cleveland School of Art.

"Contemporary American Art Exhibition," 1939 New York World's Fair, Flushing Meadow, New York, June 1–July 3 (*Torso of a Dancer*).

"National Sculpture Exhibition," Whitney Museum of Art, New York, April 2–May 2. Catalogue, foreword by Herbert Adams (*Eve*).

"Sculpture International, Second International Exhibition of Contemporary Sculpture," Fairmount Park Art Association, Philadelphia Museum of Art, May 18–October 1. Catalogue (*Torso of a Dancer, Two Sisters*).

"One Hundred Thirty-Fifth Annual Exhibition of Painting and Sculpture," Pennsylvania Academy of Fine Arts, Philadelphia, January 28–March 3 (*Torso of a Dancer*).

"Exhibition of American Sculpture," Department of Fine Arts, Carnegie Institute, Pittsburgh (*Torso of a Dancer*).

"Fifty-First Annual Exhibition of Paintings and Sculpture," Art Institute of Chicago, November 14–January 5, 1941. Catalogue, foreword by Daniel Catton Rich (*Acrobat, Juggler, and Lovesick Clowns*).

1941

"Fifty-Second Annual Exhibition of American Paintings and Sculpture," Art Institute of Chicago, October 30–January 4, 1942. Catalogue, foreword by Daniel Catton Rich (*Moray Eel and Fish:* Honorable Mention in Sculpture).

"Exhibition of American Sculpture," Department of Fine Arts, Carnegie Institute, Pittsburgh, January 14–February 28. Catalogue (*Moray Eel and Fish*).

1942

"Adam and Eve Exhibition," Detroit Institute of Arts, March 3–31. Catalogue (*Eve*).

1945

"Annual Exhibition for Michigan Artists," Detroit Institute of Arts, November 13–December 16. Catalogue, foreword by Clyde H. Burroughs (*Siberian Ram, Bacchante*).

1946

"Annual Fine Arts Exhibition," Michigan Academy of Science, Arts, and Letters, April 12–26 (*Bacchante, Portrait of a Japanese*).

"Michigan Painters, Sculptors and Craftsmen," Alger House, Detroit Institute of Arts, August 1–September 22 (*Kneeling Figure; Eve; Acrobat, Juggler, and Heartsick Clowns*).

"Annual Exhibition for Michigan Artists," Detroit Institute of Arts, November 12–December 15. Catalogue, foreword by Clyde H. Burroughs (*Eve: David B. Werbe Memorial Prize; Moray Eel and Fish*).

"Origins of Modern Sculpture," Detroit Institute of Arts, January 22–March 3.

1947

"Annual Exhibition for Michigan Artists," Detroit Institute of Arts, November 11–December 14 (*Baboon and Friend*).

1948

"Annual Exhibition for Michigan Artists," Detroit Institute of Arts, November 12–December 12. Catalogue, foreword by Edgar P. Richardson (*Lord Byron*).

"Second Exhibition of Work in Progress in Michigan," Detroit Institute of Arts, November 23–December 21 (*La Penseuse [The Thinker]; Head of a Japanese; Acrobat, Juggler, and Lovesick Clowns; Clown [Circus Clown]; Fish [Japanese Goldfish], Frog, Lizard;* and photographs of three architectural reliefs commissioned for government buildings).

"Exhibition for Michigan Craftsmen," Detroit Institute of Arts, April 6–May 4.

1949

"The Modern Artist and His World," Denver Art Museum, March 6–April 27. Educational Brochure.

"Annual Exhibition for Michigan Artists," Detroit Institute of Arts, December 13–January 15, 1950. Catalogue, foreword by Edgar P. Richardson (*Memorial Eagle [American Eagle]*).

"Michigan Works in Progress," Saginaw Museum, Saginaw, Michigan (*Bacchante, La Penseuse [The Thinker]*).

"Annual Exhibition for Michigan Artist-Craftsmen," Detroit Institute of Arts, March 15–April 10 (two medals).

1950

Exhibition, Michigan Academy of Science, Arts, and Letters (sketches for *Limestone No. 1* and *No. 2; Young Knight:* Academy Award of Merit).

"Modern Sculpture," Museum of the Cranbrook Academy of Art, Bloomfield Hills, Michigan, October 14–November 27 (*Acrobat, Juggler, and Lovesick Clowns*).

1951

"Michigan Artists 1901–1951 in Commemoration of Detroit's 250th Birthday," Detroit Institute of Arts, April 8–September 16 (*Eve*).

Exhibition of photographs of sculpture in relation to contemporary architecture, American Institute of Architects, Washington, D.C., April 29–May 19. Solo Exhibition.

"Annual Exhibition for Michigan Artists, Commissions for Michigan Artists," Detroit Institute of Arts, November 15–December 16. Catalogue, foreword by Edgar P. Richardson (*Childhood Friends*, *The Romance of Transportation*, and photographs of recent commissions).

1952

"Forty-Third Annual Exhibition for Michigan Artists," Detroit Institute of Arts, November 18–December 21. Catalogue, foreword by Edgar P. Richardson (*Warrior Saint*).

"Work in Progress in Michigan, Exhibition of the Michigan Sculpture Society," Detroit Institute of Arts, September 14–October 12 (*Don Quixote).*

"Art Corner Show, The Works of Marshall Fredericks," Woman's City Club of Detroit. Solo Exhibition.

1953

"Integration: The Use of Painting and Sculpture with Architecture in Daily Life," Contemporary Art Museum, Houston, November 8–December 6. Catalogue, foreword by Frank Dolejska, essay on "Architecture and Sculpture" by Marshall Fredericks (photographs of *Victory Eagle*).

"Forty-Fourth Annual Exhibition for Michigan Artists," Detroit Institute of Arts, November 17–December 20. Catalogue, foreword by Edgar P. Richardson (*Sun Worshipper*).

1954

"The Sculptor Draws," Peggy DeSalle's Little Gallery, Birmingham, Michigan. Solo Exhibition.

"Forty-Fifth Annual Exhibition for Michigan Artists," Detroit Institute of Arts, November 16–December19. Catalogue, foreword by Edgar P. Richardson (*Don Quixote*).

1955

"Forty-Sixth Annual Exhibition for Michigan Artists, Commissions for Michigan Artists" Detroit Institute of Arts, November 15–December18. Catalogue, foreword by Edgar P. Richardson.

"Michigan Art through Fifty Years: A Loan Exhibition for the University of Michigan," University of Michigan Museum of Art, Ann Arbor, Michigan (*Two Sisters*).

"Honor Awards and Michigan Craftsmen Exhibition," American Institute of Architects, September 21–October 16.

1956

"Architectural Design and Its Related Arts," L'école nationale supérieure d'architecture et les arts décoratifs, Brussels, exchange exhibition sponsored by the Architectural League of New York. Catalogue (*The Family Protected by Healing Herbs* [photograph]).

"Forty-Seventh Annual Exhibition for Michigan Artists, Commissions for Michigan Artists," Detroit Institute of Arts, November13–December 23 (*The Lion and Mouse*).

1957

"American Institute of Architects Sculpture Competition," Detroit Chapter (Second Prize).

1958

"One Hundred Fifty-Third Annual Exhibition, American Painting and Sculpture," Pennsylvania Academy of the Fine Arts, Philadelphia, January 26–February 23, in collaboration with the Detroit Institute of Arts, March 18–April 13. Catalogue, foreword by Edgar P. Richardson (*Saints and Sinners*).

1959

Kingswood School, Cranbrook Art Gallery, Bloomfield Hills, Michigan. Solo Exhibition.

1961

"The Court of Honor," National Exchange Club, Toledo, Ohio. Catalogue (*Birth of the Atomic Age*).

1963

"Michigan Art: Yesterday and Today," Flint Institute of Arts, Flint, Michigan, April 11–May 5. Catalogue, foreword by Stuart Hodge (*Siberian Ram*).

1966

"Sixth Annual Exhibition: American Sculpture 1900–1965," Flint Institute of Arts, Flint, Michigan (*Torso of a Dancer*).

1977

"Art in Architecture," Meadow Brook Art Gallery, Oakland University, Rochester, Michigan, January 23–March 13. Catalogue (sculptural study of *Harlequin*s for Henry and Edsel Ford Auditorium).

"The Public Monument and Its Audience," Cleveland Museum of Art, December 13–March 8, 1978. Catalogue by Marianne Doezema and June Hargrove (preliminary presentation models for the *Cleveland War Memorial: Peace Arising from the Flames of War*)

"Fédération Internationale de la Médaille (F.I.D.E.M.)," Florence, Italy (Brookgreen Gardens *Leaping Gazelle Medal*).

1989

"One Hundred Sixty-Fourth Annual Exhibition," National Academy of Design, New York, February 10–March 26. Catalogue (*Flying Wild Geese*).

"Michigan Outdoor Sculpture II Exhibition," Southfield Civic Center, September 14–November 14. Catalogue (*Flying Wild Geese*).

"Remembering the Future: The New York World's Fair from 1939–1964," Queens Museum, Flushing Meadow-Corona Park, New York. Catalogue (model for *Freedom of the Human Spirit*).

1990

"CastExpo '90: Art of Casting/Casting Art," Detroit Focus Gallery, sponsored by the American Foundrymen's Society, Inc. (*Don Quixote, The Thinker*).

"Milles as Mentor," Cranbrook Art Museum, Bloomfield Hills, Michigan, May 21–December 2 (*Night* and *Day, Leaping Gazelle*).

1991

"The Cranbrook Collection: New and Notable Acquisitions, 1989–1991," Cranbrook Art Museum, Bloomfield Hills, Michigan, June 9–October 27 (*Persephone*).

1992

"1992 Permanent Exhibit Collection," Muskegon Museum of Art, Muskegon, Michigan (*Leaping Gazelle*).

Millesgården, Lidingö, Sweden (*Leaping Gazelle*).

1993

"One Hundred Years of American Sculpture," National Sculpture Society, Americas Tower, New York, September 22–February 25, 1994 (*Siberian Ram*).

1994

"The Sculpture of Marshall Fredericks: A Tribute," Cranbrook Art Museum, Bloomfield Hills, Michigan, November 16–January 29, 1995. Solo Exhibition. Brochure text by Michael Panhorst (*Torso of a Dancer, Leaping Gazelle, Clowns, Sun Worshipper, Siberian Ram, Don Quixote de la Mancha, Baboon and Friend I* and *II [Baboon and Sleeping Child* and *Baboon and Friend], Lord Bryon, Saints and Sinners, The Friendly Dragon, Pro Patria, Guardian Angel,* and photographs).

"The Romance of Transportation: Vehicle and Voyage in North American Art," Michigan Artrain. Catalogue by Nan Plummer (*Modern Transportation [Modern Trains]* and large transparency of *The Romance of Transportation*).

"Marshall Fredericks: An Exhibition of His Sculpture," Robert L. Kidd Associates/Galleries, Birmingham, Michigan, November 10–December 3. Solo Exhibition.

"Sculpture on the Grand," Gerald R. Ford Museum, Grand Rapids, Michigan, presented by Frederik Meijer Gardens, September 7–April 1995 (*Two Bears, The Boy and Bear, The Friendly Dragon[s], The Friendly Frog, Nordic Swan, Flying Wild Geese, Night and Day, Wings of the Morning*.

1995

"Twentieth Anniversary National Sculpture Exhibition," Lyme Academy of Fine Arts, Old Lyme, Connecticut, December 16–February 4, 1996. Catalogue (*Persephone*).

"Our Town Exhibition," Birmingham Community House, Birmingham, Michigan, October 18–22. Catalogue (*Baboon and Friend I:* First Place; *Otter*).

Permanent exhibition of sixty-two photographs of sculpture installed in conjunction with *God on the Rainbow (Gud Fader På Himmelsbågen)*, Nacka Strand, Sweden.

1996

"American Masters: Sculpture from Brookgreen Gardens," Brookgreen Gardens, Pawleys Island, South Carolina, April 1996–May 1998 (*Wings of the Morning, Persephone*).

"Fifth Annual Meadow Brook Hall Landscape and Garden Show," Rochester, Michigan, (*Baboon Playing a Mandolin, Flying Wild Geese, Grouse, Hawk, Moray Eel and Fish, Otter, Rabbit, Siberian Ram, Sun Worshipper*).

"The Scarab Club Portfolio," City Gallery, Dearborn, Michigan, October 24–November 21 (*Sun Worshipper*).

"The Creation and Conservation of *The Expanding Universe* Fountain at the Department of State Building," Washington, D.C., organized by Marshall M. Fredericks Sculpture Museum, Saginaw Valley State University (models for *The Expanding Universe, Fountain of Eternal Life, Freedom of the Human Spirit, The Spirit of Detroit*, drawing, and photographs).

"Our Town Exhibition," Birmingham Community House, Birmingham, Michigan, October 23–27. Catalogue (*Sun Worshipper*: Sponsor's Award; *Rabbit*).

1997

"Artwalk Royal Oak," Royal Oak Arts Council and the Royal Oak Gallery Association, Royal Oak, Michigan (*Star Dream Fountain*).

Bay Harbor, Petoskey, Michigan. Solo Exhibition.

"Monumental Cleveland: Preserving a Sculptural Heritage," Cleveland State University (model for *Cleveland War Memorial: Fountain of Eternal Life*).

"The Sixth Annual Meadow Brook Hall Landscape and Garden Show," Rochester, Michigan (*Baboon and Friend, Baboon Playing a Mandolin, Leaping Gazelle, Siberian Ram, Sun Worshipper*).

1998

"Artists of the Scarab Club," Arts Midland, Midland, Michigan, January 10–March 22 (*Steers*).

"Stages of Creation: Public Sculptures by National Academicians," National Academy of Design, New York, January 7–March 8 (model for *The Expanding Universe* and photographs).

"American Masters: Sculpture from Brookgreen Gardens," traveling exhibition: Jack S. Blanton Museum of Art, University of Texas, Austin, June 12–August 16; Terra Museum of American Art, Chicago, January 16–April 18, 1999; National Sculpture Society, New York, May 10–July 30, 1999; Tampa Museum of Art, Tampa, Florida, September 5–October 31, 1999. Catalogue, foreword by Robin R. Salmon (*Persephone*).

"How Sculpture Is Made," Frederik Meijer Gardens and Sculpture Park, Grand Rapids, Michigan, August 29–November 15 (*The Friendly Dragon[s]*).

1999

"Masterworks of American Sculpture: Selections from Members of the National Sculpture Society," Fleischer Museum, Scottsdale, Arizona, October 20–May 2000 (model for *The Expanding Universe*, historical photographs).

2000

"Envisioning the Divine: The Religious and Spiritual Works of Marshall Fredericks," Frederik Meijer Gardens and Sculpture Park, Grand Rapids, Michigan, September 17–March 1, 2001. Solo Exhibition (*Sun Worshipper, The Spirit of Detroit, Grape and Vine, Saints and Sinners, Christ the Good Shepherd, Sheep, Christ on the Cross, Angel in the Hand of God, Eve*).

"Exploring American Sculpture," Brookgreen Gardens, Pawleys Island, South Carolina (*Two Bears*; photograph of work in progress).

2001

"Island in the City: Belle Isle," an exhibition in honor of Detroit's Tricentennial, Detroit Historical Society, March 23–September 9. Companion book by Janet Anderson, with essay by Michael Panhorst (photograph of *Levi L. Barbour Memorial Fountain*, small-scale *Leaping Gazelle*).

"Marshall Fredericks: Sculpture," Krasl Art Center, St. Joseph, Michigan, October 5–November 18. Solo Exhibition (featuring the 10 commemorative campaign posthumous castings from the Marshall M. Fredericks Sculpture Museum: *The Spirit of Detroit, Circus Clown, Two Bears, The Thinker, Leaping Gazelle, The Boy and Bear, Siberian Ram, Flying Wild Geese, American Eagle [Ann Arbor War Memorial Eagle]*, and *Mouse*; rough bronze casting of *Torso of a Dancer*; two life drawings: female nude kneeling and female nude reclining;a selection of the artist's tools, and photographs).

2002

"Allow the Spirit to Soar: Tribute to Marshall M. Fredericks," Birmingham Historical Society at the Birmingham Historical Museum, Birmingham, Michigan, June 1–July 15, 2002 (commemorative campaign posthumous castings of *The Spirit of Detroit, Leaping Gazelle, The Boy and Bear, The Thinker, Circus Clown, Mouse, Two Bears*, a selection of tools, and photographs).

"Michigan Master: Commemorative Sculptures by Marshall M. Fredericks", Saginaw Art Museum, Saginaw, Michigan, September 5–October 27, 2002 (commemorative campaign posthumous castings of *The Spirit of Detroit, Leaping Gazelle, The Boy and Bear, The Thinker, Circus Clown, Mouse, Siberian Ram, Ann Arbor War Memorial Eagle, Two Bears*, and *Flying Wild Geese*).

Selected Bibliography

Archival Resources

The Marshall M. Fredericks Papers, Marshall M. Fredericks Sculpture Museum, Saginaw Valley State University, University Center, Michigan: Photographs, books, journals and articles, lectures, writings, brochures, interview transcripts, audiovisuals, exhibition catalogs, casting and project records, business and personal correspondence, awards, Danish consular and Scandinavian activity correspondence, documents relating to ICD, DIADEM, and other philanthropic activities.

Archives of American Art: Photographs, interview transcript, audiovisuals, sculpture inventory, correspondence with Edgar P. Richardson, William Mathewson Milliken, and Frank N. Wilcox.

Cranbrook Archives and *Cranbrook Art Museum,* Cranbrook Educational Community, Bloomfield Hills Michigan: Photographs, journals and articles, interview transcripts, audiovisuals, exhibition records, campus sculpture inventory, awards.

Brookgreen Gardens, Pawleys Island, South Carolina: Photographs, board correspondence.

Cleveland Museum of Art: Journals and articles, exhibition catalogs.

National Sculpture Society, New York: Photographs, journals and articles, audiovisuals, awards.

New York Public Library: Documentation of 1939 and 1964 New York World's Fairs.

Royal Swedish Library, Stockholm, Sweden: Correspondence with Carl Milles.

Writings by Marshall M. Fredericks

"The Availability of Talent for Various and Specific Uses." Manuscript, n.d.

"Architecture and Sculpture." *Journal of the American Institute of Architects* (July 1952): 6–8.

"Architecture and Sculpture." In *Integration: The Use of Painting and Sculpture with Architecture in Daily Life,* 12–15. Houston: Contemporary Arts Museum, 1953.

"Credo." 1955.

"The Fourth Dimension." Speech to the Prismatic Club, 1977.

"I Believe . . ." Poem about personal belief in God.

"Import of Sculptural Work" and "Meaning of the Seven Pylons." *Michigan Architect and Engineer* 25 (April 1950): 10–11.

Letter to the *Cleveland Press* explaining the meaning behind the revised model for the Cleveland War Memorial Fountain, April 16, 1951.

"The Opportunity in Ecclesiastical Art." Manuscript, n.d.

"Recollections of My First Meeting with Carl Milles—June 1930," In *Ten American Sculptors—Carl Milles' Students at Cranbrook.* Foreword by Stéffan Carlen. Companion book to an exhibition held June 3–August 31, 1986, Millesgården, Lidingö, Sweden.

"The Relation between Architecture and Sculpture." Paper presented at the Ann Arbor Conference on Esthetic Evaluation, College of Architecture and Design, University of Michigan, April 1948.

"Thoughts About the Universality of Art." Manuscript, n.d.

"The Triumph of the Human Spirit." Early description of Cleveland War Memorial project, c. 1946.

Books

Baldon, Cleo, and Ib Melchior. *Festlige Tin og Trapper* (Steps and stairways). New York: Rizzoli International Publications, Inc., 1989.

Barrie, Dennis. Introduction to *Artists in Michigan 1900–1976.* Detroit: Wayne State University Press, 1989.

Campen, Richard N. *Outdoor Sculpture in Ohio.* Chagrin Falls, Ohio: West Summit Press, 1980.

Clark, Kenneth. *The Nude: A Study in Ideal Form,* Princeton, N.J.: Princeton University Press, 1972.

Clark, Robert Judson et al. *Design in America: The Cranbrook Vision, 1925–1950,* New York: Harry N. Abrams, 1983.

Dearborn: Fifty Years of Progress. Dearborn, Mich.: Dearborn Historical Museum, 1979.

Fedderson, Christian T. *Scandinavians in Michigan,* Hancock, Mich.: The Book Concern, 1968.

Fielding, Mantle. *Dictionary of American Painters, Sculptors and Engravers.* Revised edition edited by Glen B. Opitz. Temecula, Calif.: Reprint Services Corporation, 1994.

Fisher, Marcy Heller. *Marshall M. Fredericks, Sculptor: Birmingham, Bloomfield and Beyond, A Photographic Album,* Birmingham, Mich.: Birmingham Public Schools Community Education, 1995.

___. *The Outdoor Museum: The Magic of Michigan's Marshall M. Fredericks.* Detroit: Wayne State University Press, 2001.

Goode, James M. *The Outdoor Sculpture of Washington, D.C.* Washington, D.C.: Smithsonian Institution Press, 1974.

Hoffman, Malvina. *Sculpture Inside and Out,* New York: Bonanza Books, 1939.

Hornung, Clarence P. *The American Eagle in Art and Design.* New York: Dover Publications, 1978.

Howlett, D. Roger. *The Sculpture of Donald de Lue: Gods, Prophets and Heroes.* Boston: David R. Godine, 1990.

Keller, Martha R., and Michael J. Curtis. *Public Art in Ann Arbor and Washtenaw County.* Ann Arbor: Alexa Lee Gallery, 1995.

Kipps, Kennedy. *Brookgreen Gardens.* Pawleys Island, S.C.: Wyrick and Co., 1999.

Kiska, Tim. *Detroit's Powers and Personalities.* Rochester, Mich.: Momentum Books, 1989.

Lamm, Michael. *Chevrolet 1955: Creating the Original.* Stockton, Calif.: Lamm-Morada Inc.,1991.

Mayer, A. Hyatt. Introduction to *A Century of American Sculpture: Treasures from Brookgreen Gardens.* New York: Abbeville Press, 1988.

Movimenti artistici contemporanei e maestri di pittura. Salsomaggiore Terme (Parma): Accademia Italia, 1983.

Nawrocki, Dennis Alan. *Art in Detroit Public Places.* Rev. ed. Detroit: Wayne State University Press, 1999.

Panhorst, Michael. "Levi Barbour Fountain: The Process of Creating Art." In *Island in the City: How Belle Isle Changed Detroit Forever,* compiled by Janet Anderson. Companion book to an exhibition held at the Detroit Historical Museum, March 23–September 9, 2001.

Park, Marlene, and Gerald Markowitz. *Democratic Vistas: Post Offices and Public Art in the New Deal.* Philadelphia: Temple University Press, 1984.

Plummer, Ellen A., and Frederick W. Mayer. *Outdoor Sculpture: The University of Michigan, Ann Arbor Campus.* Ann Arbor, Mich.: University of Michigan Planner's Office, 1991.

Robertson, John D. *A Pictorial History of Chevrolet: 1955–1957.* Sidney, Ohio: Amos Press, 1999.

Salmon, Robin R. *Brookgreen Gardens Sculpture: Volume II.* Pawleys Island, S.C.: Brookgreen Gardens, 1993.

Shapiro, Michael. *Bronze Casting and American Sculpture 1850–1980.* The American Art Series. Newark: University of Delaware Press, 1985.

Schoenfeld, Franziska. *The Impatient Otter.* Bloomfield Hills, Mich.: Cranbrook Press, 1998.

Sommers, Lawrence M. *Atlas of Michigan.* Lansing: Michigan State University Press, 1977.

The Story of the Ohio Union Reliefs. Columbus, Ohio: Ohio State University, [c. 1950].

Stokes, Charlotte. *Bronze Ladies, Corporate Giants, Saints and Sinners: Public Art in Oakland County.* Odyssey Research Monographs 3, no. 1. Rochester, Mich.: Oakland University, 1991.

Journals, Abstracts and Articles

Abatt, Corinne. "A Quiet Artist Leaves Giant Footprints." *Birmingham-Bloomfield Eccentric,* May 12, 1983.

"Alvin Macauley Memorial." *American Art in Stone* (October 1955): 5.

"An Engineering Art." *Friends* (March 1948): 8–9.

"Anonymity of a World-Famous Sculptor." *Tribune* (Royal Oak, Mich.), October 5, 1985.

"Architecture and the Allied Arts—Theme for ASO Convention This Fall." *Ohio Architect* 8 (July 1950): 9.

"Art—Architect's Choice." *Newsweek,* July 7, 1952, 53.

"ASO Convention Program Shapes Up." *Ohio Architect* (August 1959): 17-18.

"Barbour Memorial Fountain, Belle Isle Park, Detroit." *Art Instruction* 2 (June 1938): 2.

Baulch, Vivian M. "Marshall Fredericks—The Spirit of Detroit." *Rearview Mirror* (Detroit News Online Magazine), n.d.

Birkenhauer, Tracey. "Life's Art, Marshall Fredericks's Heart Belongs to His Work." *The Oakland Press,* November 30, 1994.

Brandeis, Adele. "Kentucky Sculpted from Life." *The Courier-Journal Magazine,* April 18, 1942, 21–24.

"Bronzes for Exteriors." *National Sculpture Review* 12 (Fall 1963): 20–21.

"Business and the Arts." *National Sculpture Review* 20 (Winter 1971–72): 20–21.

Chessler, Suzanne. "Sculptured Dreamers." *Daily Tribune* (Royal Oak, Mich.) December 15, 1994.

Clark, Kenneth. "The Naked and the Nude." *National Sculpture Review* 22 (Fall 1973): 14–17.

Coir, Mark. "Shaping the Heart of Detroit: The Saarinens' Plans for the Waterfront." Brochure for exhibition held at the Cranbrook Art Museum, June 2–September 30, 2001.

Colby, Joy Hakanson. "Interview: Marshall Fredericks Talks About His 'Dream.'" *Detroit News,* June 10, 1997.

___. "The Dragons of Marshall Fredericks: Meeting the Challenge of Metal and Stone." *Detroit News Michigan Magazine,* February 28, 1982, 12–13, 16–17, 22.

"Collaboration of Arts and Architecture Feature of Exhibition." *Monthly Bulletin, Michigan Society of Architects, The American Institute of Architects* 5 (December 1951): 51.

Couch, Frank L. "The Elementary School of Today." *Monthly Bulletin, Michigan Society of Architects, The American Institute of Architects* 24 (December 1950): 12–22.

"Cranbrook's Contribution to the 'World of Tomorrow.'" *Academy News* (May 1939).

"Dedicated to the Veterans Memorial Building, Detroit, Michigan." *Michigan Architect and Engineer* 25 (April 1950): 3–13, plates 30–32, 37.

"Detroit Civic Center Begins to Grow." *Architectural Record* (January 1951): 100–107.

Dobberowsky, Lisa. "Marshall Fredericks Made Monumental Contributions to Detroit." *DAC News* (Detroit Athletic Club) 85 (January 2000): 26–27

Dorazio, Arthur. "Sculpture by the Ton." *Detroit Free Press Sunday Graphic,* October 17, 1948, 2–4.

___. "Transportation: Story in Sculpture—From Paper to Aluminum." *Detroit Free Press Sunday Graphic,* May 20, 1951.

Dunitz, Nancy Beth. "A Guide to the Outdoor Sculptures on the University of Michigan Campus." Paper, University of Michigan, July 1980. MFSM Archives.

"Eaton Dedicates World War II Memorials at Seven Plants." *The Eaton News* (corporate newsletter) 11 (September 1949): 8.

Erbe, Jack. "Fountains Are Beautiful." *National Sculpture Review* 22 (Winter 1973–74): 23–26.

"Fine Arts Medal Awarded to Detroit Sculptor." *Michigan Architect and Engineer* 27 (June 1952): 23–24.

Fisher, Marcy. "Photo Safari Captures Fredericks's Treasures." *Update, SOS! Save Outdoor Sculpture Newsletter* 9 (Spring 1998):15.

"Flexibility—Keynotes New Administration Building for University of Michigan." *Weekly Bulletin, Michigan Society of Architects, The American Institute of Architects* 22 (October 11, 1949): 3–9.

"Fountain of Eternal Life." *Impresario* 4 (Fall 1964): 28–29.

Genauer, Emily. "Super-Sculpture." *New York Herald Tribune This Week Magazine,* September 5, 1954, 9.

Goldner, Elizabeth. "Sculptor Marshall Fredericks—Inspiring Works Are Available to All Who Live in Birmingham." *Downtown Birmingham* (Spring 1997).

Gruen, Victor. "Art and Architecture." *Stone* 78 (November 1958): 12–13, 22.

Haight, Jeffrey M. "Saints and Sinners." Paper, Oakland University, Rochester, Mich., November 1985. MFSM Archives.

Hakanson (Colby), Joy. "Detroit Is His Studio." *Detroit News Sunday Pictorial Magazine,* October 26, 1958, 7–9.

___. "Fiberglass Sculpture." *Detroit News Sunday Pictorial Magazine,* April 26, 1953, 6–7.

Harris, N. Neil, and Pat Black. "A Loving Tribute to Sculptors: Brookgreen Gardens, A Personal View." *The Numismatist* (June 1981): 1468–92.

Horn, Milton. "Five Sculptors of the Midwest." *National Sculpture Review* 27 (Spring 1978): 8–13.

"Indian River Shrine, Alden B. Dow, F.A.I.A., Architect." *Monthly Bulletin, Michigan Society of Architects, The American Institute of Architects* (August 1959): 27.

Iorio, Mary E. "A Monumental Life." *Cranbrook Journal* (Summer 1995): 2–9.

Jensen, Oluf. "Marshall Fredericks, Sculptor." *The Nordic News* 51 (February 1981).

Journal of the Royal Architectural Institute of Canada 33 (June 1956): 229.

"Kids Go on Fredericks Art Safari." *Birmingham-Bloomfield Eccentric,* January 26, 1995.

Klemic, Mary. "Perspectives: Fredericks Exhibit Shares Inspiration." *Birmingham-Bloomfield Eccentric,* January 19, 1995.

___. "Sculptor Shows Sensitive Touch." *Birmingham-Bloomfield Eccentric,* November 17, 1994.

Kraft, Tone. "Norsemen Abroad—Marshall Fredericks of Giant Sculptures." *The Norseman* 4 (1965): 117–120.

Lantz, Michael. "Public Sculpture . . . The Talk of the Town." *National Sculpture Review* 31 (Spring 1982): 22–23.

___. "Seventy-Seven Approaches to Sculpture." *National Sculpture Review* 32 (Winter 1983–84): 10–15.

Little, Sybil. "A Monumental Sculptor: Life Stories of Artist Stand as Tall as His Work." *Oakland Press,* March 2, 1997.

Maloney, S. C. "Marshall Fredericks's Monument to Christ." *Birmingham Town Hall Magazine* 9 (Spring 1960): 10–11.

"Man of the Expanding Universe." *National Sculpture Review* 45 (Spring 1997): 35.

"Marshall Fredericks's Artistic Fulfillment." *Birmingham Town Hall Magazine* (Fall 1956): 19–23.

"Marshall Fredericks's Expanding Universe." *Impresario* 3 (Winter 1964): 12.

"Marshall Fredericks Honored with American Achievement Award." *Brookgreen Journal* 27 (1977): 4–5.

"Marshall M. Fredericks Creating in Bronze." *American Dane* (Sept. 1979): 12.

Mc Clean, Evelyn G. "Marshall M. Fredericks, K. D.—Sculptor." *University of Windsor Review* 6 (Spring 1971): 29–45.

McCay, David. "Miracle in a Bean Field." *Detroit Free Press,* November 6, 1990.

Merk-Gould, Linda. "Preserving the Artist's Intent: From Which Decade? Marshall Fredericks's Cleveland War Memorial Fountain." *Abstracts of Papers Presented at the Twentieth Annual Meeting, American Institute for Conservation of Historic and Artistic Works,* Washington, D.C. (June 2–7, 1992):14.

"Modern Furniture for Anthropoids." *Life,* June 20, 1955, 59–60, 62.

"The New York World's Fair 1939." *New York Times Special Supplement* (Fall 1939).

"New York World's Fair." *American Art Today.* Poughkeepsie, N.Y.: *Apollo* magazine, 1987.

Noble, Joseph Veach. "Dawn of a New Day: 1939/1940 New York World's Fair." *National Sculpture Review* 29 (Fall 1980): 22–24.

"Ornamental Aluminum Castings." *Modern Metals* 22 (April 1966): 36, 38.

Panhorst, Michael W. "Artists' Intent for Monumental Twentieth-Century Outdoor Bronze Sculptures in the United States." *Abstracts of Papers Presented at the Twenty-Second Annual Meeting, American Institute for Conservation of Historic and Artistic Works,* Washington, D.C. (June 6–11, 1994).

___. "Cleveland's Fountain of Eternal Life Gets 99-Year Lease on Life." *Cultural Resources Management* 18 (1995): 38–40.

___. "Marshall M. Fredericks: A Monumental Passion for Life." *Scandinavian Review* (1998): 40–46.

___. "Uncovering Artists' Intent for Twentieth-Century Outdoor Bronze Sculptures. *Update, SOS! Save Outdoor Sculpture Newsletter* 11 (Spring 2000): 20–22.

Pasfield, Veronica. "Marshall Fredericks." *Detroit Monthly* (November 1992): 64–69, 89.

Pejtersen, Ole C. [Marshall Fredericks, Sculptor, World Class Artist] translation. *Danmarks Posten* 3 (June 1986).

"Please Climb the Bears!" *Christian Science Monitor,* January 13, 1967.

"Presenting the Horace Rackham Educational Memorial." *The Foundation, Dedication Issue* (January 1942): 8ff.

Proske, Beatrice Gilman. "Brookgreen Gardens Golden Anniversary." *National Sculpture Review* 30 (Spring 1981): 16–19.

Provenzano, Frank. "Touched by Greatness." *Birmingham-Bloomfield Eccentric,* February 16, 1998, sec. C, 1.

Putnam, Beatrice Morgan, photographer. "Dynamic Detroit." Industrial Publishing Corporation of Detroit, n.d.

"Recent Dedications." *National Sculpture Review* 11 (Winter 1962–63): 14–15.

"Renovated Sculpture Rededicated at State." *State Magazine* (United States Department of State) (January-February 1997).

Salmon, Robin R. "Brookgreen Gardens, Sculpture, Nature, Beauty . . ." *National Sculpture Review* 40, no. 2 (1991): 20–27.

___. "Marshall Fredericks: Dean of American Sculptors." *Brookgreen Journal* 25 (1995): 2–7.

Sawyer, Sally. "Marshall Fredericks, Sculptor." *Detroit Home Journal*, November 17, 1983.

"Sculptor Marks Ford's 50th Year." *Ford Times* (February 1953): 48–49.

"Sculpture at the New York World's Fair." *National Sculpture Review* 13 (Summer 1964): 16–17.

Selden, Florence. "Michigan's Trailblazing Sculptor." *Inside Michigan* 3 (August 1953): 36.

"The Shrine." *Graphic Resorter* (Petoskey, Mich.), August 27, 1979, 5–6.

Smith, Terrence. "Marshall Fredericks: Multi-talented Man." *The Daily News* (Greenville, Mich.), August 16, 1985.

Southwell, William. "Examining the Divine/Human Nature of Christ." *National Sculpture Review* 36, no. 4 (1978): 14–15.

"*Spirit of Detroit* Arrives via Seaway." *Trucking News* (October 1958): 14–15, 24–25.

"*Spirit of Detroit* Greets President in Motor City." *New York Times*, October 18, 1960.

Stasak, Marv. "Quiet! Sculptor at Work." *Birmingham Eccentric*, August 18, 1960.

Stirton, Malcolm R. "In Honor of Those Who Gave Their Lives for Their Country." *Monthly Bulletin, Michigan Society of Architects, The American Institute of Architects* 24 (October 1950): 7–16.

"Stone." *Art and Architecture* 78 (November 1958): 13, 22, 24.

"Ten Sculptures of Marshall M Fredericks." *Pencil Points* 20 (May 1939): 2, 61–64.

"The Work of Marshall M. Fredericks." *Monthly Bulletin, Michigan Society of Architects, The American Institute of Architects* (June 1956): 20–38.

"To Lift the Spirit." *American Dane* (June 1973): 4–5, 7.

"Voices of Northeast Ohio." *Forbes FYI Magazine* (Winter 2000): 12–13.

Walker, Ralph. "The Levi L. Barbour Memorial Fountain." *Pencil Points* 18 (February 1937): 92–95.

Watson, Ernest W. "Sculptor to the People, Marshall Fredericks." *American Artist* 18 (September 1954): 36–40, 67–70.

Weisberg, Gabriel P. "The Educational Thematic Exhibitions at the Cleveland Museum of Art." *School Arts* (April 1979): 12–14.

Audiovisual

Brookgreen Gardens. Informational video produced by Austin Kelley Adv., Inc., 1997. 8 min. VHS.

Carl Milles: God on the Rainbow. Produced by Deitrich H. Müller, NTSC, 1995. 6 min.VHS.

Celebrate the Spirit. Produced by the Marshall M. Fredericks Sculpture Gallery, Saginaw Valley State University, University Center, Michigan, 1992. 7 min. VHS.

Christ on the Cross (segment one). "Michigan Magazine," television program, 1991. 13 min. VHS.

Christ on the Cross (segment two). "Michigan Magazine," television program, 1992. 15 min. VHS.

The Chrysler Art Collection: Interview with Marshall Fredericks. Produced by the Chrysler Corporation, 1996. 55 min. VHS.

Cleveland: The Fountain of Eternal Life, 1960. Archival footage. 16 mm.

Colby, Joy Hakanson. *Marshall Fredericks, Interview, August 5, 1981.* Archives of American Art Oral History Program. Audiocassette. Transcript available from MFSM.

Conservation Planning Meeting for the Expanding Universe Fountain: Interview with Marshall Fredericks. Professional Services Branch, GSA, State Dept., 1993. 29 min. VHS.

Cranbrook Academy of Art Museum, c. 1940–42. Archival footage. 41 min. Film transferred to VHS. Cranbrook Archives.

Eidelberg, Martin, J. Farmer, Joan Marter, and Davira Taragin. *Interview with Marshall Fredericks, June 2, 1991.* Audiocassette. Transcript available from the Cranbrook Art Museum.

Fredericks, Marshall. Lecture and slide show for Cranbrook Academy of Art, Bloomfield Hills, Michigan, 1991. 90 min. VHS.

___. Lecture and slide show for the Village Club, Bloomfield Hills, Michigan, 1991. 90 min. VHS.

Friendly Dragon (work in progress at Greenhouse Studio). Produced by Heidi Peterson, May 9, 1991. 30 min. VHS.

Global Connections. Narrated by Dr. Jonathan Swift. Bloomfield (Mich.) Community Television, 1993. 27 min. VHS.

Kazansky, Maria. *The Ugly Duckling: A Musical Illustration to the Tale by Hans Christian Andersen.* Written and performed for the dedication of the *Nordic Swan and the Ugly Duckling* fountain at the Danish Embassy, Washington, D.C., 1994. Musical score.

Kowalski, B. *Marshall M. Fredericks, Interview, May 21, 1977.* Audiocassette.

Marshall Fredericks: Public Sculptor. Archives of American Art, Smithsonian Institution, 1985. 32 min. VHS.

Marshall Fredericks: Spirit in Sculpture. Produced by Scripps Howard Broadcasting, Detroit, 1987. 20 min. VHS. Transcript available.

Marshall Fredericks. Segment of "Sunday Times" television program, WJBK Detroit, 1986. 9 min. VHS. Transcript available.

Marshall M. Fredericks Sculpture Gallery. Produced and directed by Heidi Peterson. Bloomfield (Mich.) Community Television, 1993. VHS.

The Marshall M. Fredericks Sculpture Gallery at Saginaw Valley State University. " Michigan Magazine" television program, 1991. 12 min. VHS.

McMichael, Catherine. *The Seven Saints and Sinners.* Performed by the Saginaw Choral Society, Midland Camerata Singers, and Valley Wind Quintet at Saginaw Valley State University, 1998. CD.

Michigan's Great Dane—Marshall Fredericks. Narrated and produced by Dell Warner. WDIV–TV4, Detroit, 1995. 2 hours 30 minutes. VHS.

Muller, Peter Paul. *Sculptural Works Done in Collaboration with Architects.* Produced for the National Sculpture Society, 1988. Slides.

Mus, Irvin. *Expedition, Detroit: Marshall Fredericks, Sculptor.* Narrated by Frederick Hayes, produced and directed by Peter Strand. WXYZ-TV, 1959. 30 min. 16mm transferred to VHS.

Panhorst, Michael, W. *Marshall M. Fredericks: A Life in Art* (lecture at Cranbrook Art Museum). Bloomfield (Mich.) Community Television, 1993. VHS.

Plummer, Nan. *The University of Michigan: Outdoor Sculpture on Campus.* Directed by Matthew Zacharias. Planner's Office and Museum of Art, University of Michigan, Ann Arbor, 1991. VHS.

The Magic of Marshall Fredericks: The Making of The Poet—Lord Byron. Directed by Marshall Lupp. Saginaw Valley State University, University Center, Michigan, 2001. 31 min. VHS.

Sculptor Marshall Fredericks: In His Own Words. Cable 15, Southfield, Mich., 1994. 56 min. VHS.

Sculptor's Passion: One Man's Vision. Frederik Meijer Gardens, Grand Rapids, Michigan, 1998. 11^1/$_2$ min. VHS.

The Sculpture of Marshall M. Fredericks. WXYZ–TV, Detroit, c. 1970. VHS.

The Spirit of Detroit. Chrysler Corporation Motion Pictures and Detroit-Wayne Joint Building Authority, 1959. 16mm transferred to VHS.

Stavanger Leaping Gazelle, Ann Arbor War Memorial Eagle, and *Victory Eagle (Veterans Memorial Eagle).* Archival footage, c. 1959. 11 min. 16mm. transferred to VHS.

A Tribute to Marshall M. Fredericks: In Celebration of his Ninetieth Birthday at the Community House. Bloomfield (Mich.) Community Television, 1998. VHS.

Note: Television news clips from Detroit and Cleveland stations, installation and dedication footage, work-in-progress shots in the studio, the Greenhouse, and foundries, award presentations, and segments from Scandinavian occasions are also available from the archives of the Marshall M. Fredericks Sculpture Museum.

Obituaries

Colby, Joy Hakanson. "Marshall Fredericks, 'Spirit of Detroit's Sculptor." *Detroit News,* April 6, 1998.

Durbin, Dee Ann. "Death of a Dream." *Weekly Tribune Plus* (Royal Oak, Mich.), week of April 12, 1998.

___. "'Spirit of Detroit' Sculptor Marshall Fredericks Dies at 90." *Oakland Press* (Oakland County, Mich.), April 6, 1998.

Green, Roger. "Fredericks's Art Touched Generations." *Bay City Times* (Bay City, Mich.), April 12, 1998.

Hendrix, Pam. "Fountain Creator Passes Away." *Oakland Post* (Rochester, Mich.), April 8, 1998.

Montermurri, Patricia. "Sculptor Was Local; Images Were Global." *Detroit Free Press,* April 6, 1998.

Panhorst, Michael W. "Artist Never Gave Up." *Bay City Times* (Bay City, Mich.), April 12, 1998.

Sanchez, Brenna. "Marshall Fredericks: Carving Out a Spirited Vision." *Hour Detroit,* December 1998, 72–75.

Vishnevsky, Zina. "Marshall Fredericks, Created Mall A Statue." *Cleveland Plain Dealer,* April 6, 1998.

Wiswell, Joyce. "Sculptor Marshall Fredericks Dies at 90." *Mirror of Royal Oak* (Royal Oak, Mich.), April 9, 1998.

Sculpture in Public and Corporate Collections

Works cited are in bronze unless otherwise noted. An asterisk denotes smaller versions, including castings from sketches and scale models as well as later reductions.

Alden B. Dow Home and Studio, Midland, Michigan
Anniversary Baboons
Childhood Friends, relief*
*Saints and Sinners**

Alma College, Alma, Michigan
*American Eagle (Ann Arbor War Memorial Eagle)**
Flying Wild Geese

American Embassy, London, England
Great Seal of the United States (rendition), medallion, aluminum

B&O Railroad Museum, Baltimore, Maryland
The Romance of Transportation, Horse and Antique Trains, Modern Trains, reliefs, aluminum (relocated from Union Station, Fort Street, Detroit)

Baldwin Public Library, Birmingham, Michigan
Siberian Ram, limestone

Barbara Hallman Plaza, Royal Oak, Michigan
Star Dream Fountain, bronze, granite, and stainless steel

Bayview Yacht Club, Grosse Pointe, Michigan
Thunder Bay Island Light Trophy (Bayview–Mackinac Island Yacht Race Trophy)

Belle Isle, Detroit
Levi L. Barbour Memorial Fountain: Leaping Gazelle: bronze; *Grouse, Hawk, Otter,* and *Rabbit*: granite

Birger Sandzén Memorial Gallery, Lindsborg, Kansas
The Thinker

Birmingham Bloomfield Art Center, Birmingham, Michigan
*Black Elk: Homage to the Great Spirit,** posthumous casting

Birmingham Covington School, Bloomfield Hills, Michigan
Hiawatha, relief*

Birmingham Pierce Elementary School, Birmingham, Michigan
Sheep (The Guests Have Arrived), relief

Birmingham Quarton Elementary School, Birmingham, Michigan
*Two Bears**

Birmingham Seaholm High School, Birmingham, Michigan
Young Knight, German silver

Birmingham War Memorial, City Hall, Birmingham, Michigan
Great Seal of the United States Relief (rendition), gilt bronze

Brookgreen Gardens, Pawleys Island, South Carolina
Baboons, Female and *Male*
Flying Wild Geese
Gazelle Fountain
Persephone (Bacchante)
The Thinker
Two Bears
Wings of the Morning
Siberian Ram

Camp Ho-Mita-Koda, Newbury, Ohio
Playing Bears Fountain, stone

Camp Ohiyesa (YMCA), Holly, Michigan
O-HI-E-SA (Dr. Charles Eastman), relief

Central United Methodist Church, Waterford, Michigan
Christ the Good Shepherd, relief, gold anodized aluminum

Christ Church Episcopal, Grosse Pointe, Michigan
Flying Wild Geese

Christian Family Center, Adrian, Michigan
Merillat Double Portrait Plaque

Dow Chemical Company, Midland, Michigan
Willard Henry Dow, portrait relief

Dow Gardens, Midland, Michigan
Leaping Gazelle

Eastland Center, Harper Woods, Michigan
The Lion and Mouse, limestone and gilt bronze

Eaton Corporation (formerly Eaton Manufacturing
   Corporation), Cleveland, Ohio
Eaton War Memorial Eagle

Elmwood Cemetery, Detroit, Michigan
Flying Wild Geese (Alvan Macauley Memorial)

Federal Reserve Bank, Cincinnati, Ohio
Victory Eagle (American Eagle)

Ferndale Public Library, Ferndale, Michigan
*Two Bears**

First Federal of Michigan, Detroit, Michigan
*Leaping Gazelle**

First Presbyterian Church of Birmingham,
   Birmingham, Michigan
*American Eagle (Ann Arbor War Memorial Eagle)**
Flying Wild Geese Medallion, posthumous casting
*Wings of the Morning**

Flint Children's Museum, Flint, Michigan
The Friendly Frog, terrazzo with gold-plated bronze

Flushing Meadow-Corona Park, New York
Freedom of the Human Spirit

Ford Motor Company, Dearborn, Michigan
Ford Research and Engineering Memorial, relief

Foreign Ministry Building, Copenhagen, Denmark
Flying Wild Geese
The Thinker

Fox-Hills Pre-School, Bloomfield Hills, Michigan
*Two Bears**

Frederik Meijer Gardens and Sculpture Park,
   Grand Rapids, Michigan
Acrobat, Juggler and Lovesick Clowns
*American Eagle (Ann Arbor War Memorial Eagle)**
Baboon and Baby Chimpanzee
Baboon and Sitting Friend
Baboon and Sleeping Child
The Boy and Bear
Flying Wild Geese
The Friendly Dragon (2)
The Friendly Frog
Grouse
Hawk
Leaping Gazelle

*Lord Byron**
*Night and Day Fountain**
Nordic Swan and the Ugly Duckling
Otter
Rabbit
*Saints and Sinners**
Siberian Ram
The Thinker
Two Bears
Victory Eagle (American Eagle) (2)*
Wings of the Morning

Freeport, Grand Bahama Island
Sir Winston Churchill Memorial

The Gardens, Palm Beach, Florida
Leaping Gazelle

Gibbes Museum of Art, Charleston, South Carolina
Persephone (Bacchante)

Greenwood Cemetery, Birmingham, Michigan
Flying Wild Geese (Kilgour Memorial)
Leaping Gazelle (Marshall Fredericks's grave)

Grosse Pointe Public Library, Central Branch, Grosse
   Pointe, Michigan
*The Boy and Bear**

Grosse Pointe Yacht Club, Grosse Pointe, Michigan
George Mertz Slocum, portrait relief

Henry and Edsel Ford Auditorium, Detroit (currently
   closed to the public)
*The Ford Empire, Harlequins, Ballerina, Circus
   Parade*, and *Orchestral Parade*, repoussé and
   formed metals: copper, nickel, brass, stainless
   steel, and aluminum, plated with gold, zinc, and
   cadmium

Henry Ford Centennial Library, Dearborn, Michigan
*Henry Ford Memorial: Childhood, The Ford Empire,
   Formative Years, Ford Cars, Henry Ford*, bronze
   on marble

Henry Ford Museum and Greenfield Village,
   Dearborn, Michigan
Henry Ford, bust
Mercury, polished nickel (Benson Ford Research
   Center)

Henry J. McMorran Auditorium, Port Huron,
   Michigan
Night and Day Fountain
Sculptured Clock, gold anodized aluminum

Heritage Park, Greenville, Michigan
*Nordic Swan and the Ugly Duckling:
   Hans Christian Andersen Fountain*

Horace H. Rackham Educational Memorial Building, Detroit
Automotive Engineering, Chinese Astronomer, Education and Science, Knowledge, Learning, Pegasus, Primitive Education, Steelworkers, marble; and twenty-eight untitled reliefs, bronze and granite
Mary A. Rackham, portrait relief

Holy Ghost Seminary, Ann Arbor, Michigan
Holy Ghost Seminary, relief

Huron Cemetery, Highland, Michigan
McManus Memorial

Huron Valley Sinai Hospital, Commerce, Michigan
Flying Wild Geese

Indian River Catholic Shrine (Cross in the Woods), Indian River, Michigan
Christ on the Cross, figure: bronze; cross: redwood

Ingham County Circuit Court, Lansing, Michigan
Seal of the Circuit Court of Ingham County (4), wood

Interlochen Center for the Arts, Interlochen, Michigan
Alden B. Dow, portrait relief (Alden Dow Plaza)
Two Bears (Alden Dow Plaza)

Jefferson Memorial Elementary School, Wyandotte, Michigan
Childhood Friends, relief

John Ball Zoological Garden, Grand Rapids, Michigan
*Victory Eagle (American Eagle)**

John Weld Peck Federal Building, Cincinnati, Ohio
American Eagle

Kalamazoo Presbyterian Church, Kalamazoo, Michigan
*Wings of the Morning**

Kellogg Foundation, Battle Creek, Michigan
Flying Wild Geese

Kirk in the Hills Presbyterian Church, Bloomfield Hills, Michigan
Peace Arising from the Flames of War (central figure and sphere from *Fountain of Eternal Life*)*
Wings of the Morning

Krasl Art Center, St. Joseph, Michigan
Otter

Kunstmuseum, Holstelbro, Denmark
The Thinker

Lake Superior State College, Sault Ste. Marie, Michigan
Walker Lee Cisler, portrait relief

Lincoln National Life Insurance, Indianapolis, Indiana
Arthur F. Hall, portrait relief

Louisville Courier-Journal Building, Louisville, Kentucky
Spirit of Kentucky reliefs: *Huckleberry Finn and Tom Sawyer Observing the Boats and Giant Catfish; Pioneer Family and Animals of the Region; Raccoons; Riverboats and Giant Catfish; Thoroughbreds, Sheep and Tobacco Farmers*

Lucille E. Andersen Memorial Garden, Andersen Enrichment Center, Saginaw, Michigan
Flying Wild Geese

Mackinac Island Museum, Mackinac Island, Michigan
William Beaumont, M.D., portrait relief, copper-patinated bronze

Macomb County Building, Mt. Clemens, Michigan
John F. Kennedy Memorial

Madison High School, Madison Heights, Michigan
*American Eagle (Ann Arbor War Memorial Eagle)**

Marselisborg Castle, Århus, Denmark
Leaping Gazelle

Marshall M. Fredericks Sculpture Museum, Saginaw Valley State University, University Center, Michigan
Acrobat, Juggler and Lovesick Clowns
*Acrobat, Juggler and Lovesick Clowns**
Adelbert Akusy
African Mother and Child
*American Eagle (Ann Arbor War Memorial Eagle),** posthumous casting
Anniversary Baboons
Asiatic Figure
*Baboon Playing a Mandolin**
Baboons, Female and Male
*Baby Baboon**
*Black Elk: Homage to the Great Spirit**
The Boy and Bear
*The Boy and Bear**
*The Boy and Bear** posthumous casting
Celestial Fountain, two sketch models, female and male
Chimpanzee (Philosopher), relief
Christ and the Children, relief
*Christ on the Cross**
Christ the Good Shepherd, relief section of lamb, gold anodized aluminum
Circus Clown
Circus Clown, posthumous
Clown Musicians
Dexter M. Ferry, Jr., portrait relief
Don Quixote (2)
*Don Quixote,** silvered bronze
Eaton War Memorial Eagle
Eve

*The Expanding Universe (Man and the Expanding Universe)**
Flying Pterodactyls
Flying Wild Geese
*Flying Wild Geese**
*Flying Wild Geese** posthumous casting
*Fountain of Eternal Life**
*Freedom of the Human Spirit,** posthumous casting
*The Friendly Dragon**
Henry Ford, bust
Henry Ford, figure from Henry Ford Memorial*
Hiawatha
Indian and Buffalo
Japanese Goldfish, silvered bronze
Jungle Madonna and Child, driftwood on ebony
*Leaping Gazelle**
*Leaping Gazelle** posthumous casting
*Lion and Monkey**
The Lion and Mouse
Lord Byron, posthumous casting
*Lord Byron**
Lovesick Clown
The Lute Player
Mary Soper Pope Memorial Award, terracotta
Mary Queen of Scots
Modern Trains, aluminum
*Mother and Child,** gilt bronze
Motion in Nature
Motion in Nature (section)
Mouse
Mouse posthumous casting
Night and Day Fountain
Nobuji Yoshida (Portrait of a Japanese)
Nordic Swan and the Ugly Duckling
Otter
Persephone (Bacchante)
*Persephone (Bacchante)**
Pioneer Woman and Ox
Portrait of Bunichuro Sagimura
Portrait of a Chinese Actress (Chinese Girl)
Portrait of a German Philosopher
Portrait of Jean Raseman
Portrait of Marion Kirk (daughter of Arthur Neville Kirk)
Portrait of a Young Man (Lloyd Westbrook)
Portrait of an Old Man, black walnut
Portrait of Dr. William Oliver Stevens
Portrait of Vincent Anderson
Russell Barnett Aitken, terracotta
*Saints and Sinners**
Sheep (The Guests Have Arrived), relief
Siberian Ram
Siberian Ram, limestone
*Siberian Ram,** posthumous casting
Siesta (Reclining Lamb)
*Sun Worshipper**
Susanna and the Mirror, porcelain

The Spirit of Detroit
*The Spirit of Detroit**
*The Spirit of Detroit** posthumous casting
*The Spirit of Detroit,** sketch models (2)
The Thinker
*The Thinker,** posthumous casting
Torso of a Dancer
Torso of a Dancer, relief, aluminum
Trial Flight (Standing Lamb)
Two Bears
Two Bears posthumous casting
*Two Bears**
Two Sisters (Mother and Child)
*Two Sisters (Mother and Child)**
Wings of the Morning
Young Knight, German silver
Youth in the Hands of God, relief, aluminum

Meijer Inc., Grand Rapids, Michigan
Don Quixote

Michigan Medical Society, East Lansing, Michigan
Aspiration

Michigan Opera Theater, Detroit Opera House, Detroit, Michigan
Torso of a Dancer

Midland Center for the Arts, Midland, Michigan
Alden B. Dow Memorial, portrait relief
Saints and Sinners (The Seven Saints and Sinners)
*Freedom of the Human Spirit**

Millesgården, Lidingö, Sweden
*Leaping Gazelle**
The Thinker

Milliken Company, Spartanburg, North Carolina
Leaping Gazelle

Milwaukee Public Museum, Milwaukee, Wisconsin
Indian and Wild Swans, relief

Muskegon Museum of Art, Muskegon, Michigan
*Leaping Gazelle**

Nacka Strand, Sweden
God on the Rainbow (enlarged by Fredericks from a Carl Milles sketch), figures: bronze; arc: stainless steel

National City Bank, Pontiac, Michigan
Chief Pontiac, relief (head)

National Exchange Club, Toledo, Ohio
Birth of the Atomic Age, figure: aluminum; fountain: marble and granite

Nevada Art Museum, Reno, Nevada
*Two Bears**

Northwood University, Midland, Michigan
*Saints and Sinners**

Northern Michigan University, Marquette, Michigan
Flying Wild Geese

Northland Center, Southfield, Michigan
The Boy and Bear, limestone and gilt bronze

Oakland University, Rochester, Michigan
Saints and Sinners Fountain (Kresge Library)

Oakwoods Cemetery, Chicago, Illinois
Unto Thee Lift Up Mine Eyes, limestone
    (Mausoleum-Columbarium)

Ohio Bureau of Employment Services, Columbus, Ohio
*Industry and Other Employment, Recreational
    Activities*, reliefs, aluminum

Ohio Department of Transportation, Columbus,
    Ohio
Motion in Nature, Transportation by Man, reliefs,
    aluminum

Ohio State University, Columbus, Ohio
*Ceramics, Agriculture, and Aeronautical Pioneering;
    Early Pioneers and Settlers; Education and
    Government; Indians of the Ohio River Valley;
    Johnny Appleseed; The Steel Industry and River
    Freighters*, reliefs, limestone (Ohio Union Building)

Ottawa High School, Grand Rapids, Michigan
Young Knight, German silver

Our Lady of Sorrows Catholic Church, Farmington,
    Michigan
Our Lady of Sorrows Cross

Renaissance Center People Mover Station,
    Detroit, Michigan
Siberian Ram

Royal Oak Public Library, Royal Oak, Michigan
Acrobat, Juggler, and Lovesick Clowns *
*Two Bears**

Royal Palace, Stockholm, Sweden
The Thinker

Ritto, Japan
*Freedom of the Human Spirit** (Mayor's Office)

Saginaw Museum of Art, Saginaw, Michigan
Flying Wild Geese

Saginaw Valley State University, University Center,
    Michigan
Dr. Samuel D. Marble, portrait relief (Wickes Hall)
Jack McBride Ryder, portrait relief (Zahnow Library)
Leaping Gazelle Fountain
Peace Arising from the Flames of War (central figure
    and sphere from *Fountain of Eternal Life*)*

St. Hugo of the Hills, Bloomfield Hills, Michigan
Christ and the Children

St. James Episcopal Church, Birmingham, Michigan
Guardian Angel

St. John Hospital, Grosse Pointe, Michigan
Peter Austin Whyte, portrait relief

St. John's Lutheran Church, Fort Wayne, Indiana
Christ and the Children, aluminum

SBC Ameritech, Hoffman Estates, Illinois
*Acrobat Clown**
Flying Wild Geese

SBC Ameritech, Michigan Headquarters Building,
    Detroit, Michigan
*Leaping Gazelle**

Shain Park, Birmingham, Michigan
Freedom of the Human Spirit

Skaelskør, Denmark
*Nordic Swan and the Ugly Duckling:
    Hans Christian Andersen Fountain*

Smithsonian American Art Museum, Washington, D.C.
Torso of a Dancer

Southfield Civic Center, Southfield, Michigan
*Leaping Gazelle**

Southfield Public Library, Southfield, Michigan*
*Two Bears**

Starr Commonwealth, Albion, Michigan
Floyd Starr
*The Princess and the Unicorn** (Brueckner Museum)

Stavanger, Norway
Memorial to Norwegian Emigrants: Leaping Gazelle

Sterling Bank and Trust, Clawson, Michigan
*Victory Eagle (American Eagle)**

Sterling Bank and Trust, Southfield, Michigan
Black Elk: Homage to the Great Spirit, posthumous
    casting

Sterling Heights Public Library, Sterling Heights,
    Michigan
Two Bears
*Two Bears**

Toyota City, Japan
The Thinker (City Hall)
*Freedom of the Human Spirit** (Mayor's Office)
*Leaping Gazelle** (Mayor's Office)

Tracy W. McGregor Elementary School, Detroit,
    Michigan
Tracy W. McGregor, portrait relief

UAW-Ford Program Center, Detroit, Michigan
Great Seal of the United States Relief (rendition),
    gilt bronze
Victory Eagle (Veterans Memorial Eagle), marble;
    and seven carved pylons: *Battle of the Great
    Lakes; Civil War; Founding of Detroit; Indian
    Wars; Spanish-American War; World War I; Peace
    Pylon (World War II)*, marble

**United States Department of State Building,
    Washington, D.C.**
*The Expanding Universe (Man and the Expanding
    Universe) Fountain*, figure: bronze; orbit: nickel;
    basin: ceramic tile

United States Post Office, River Rouge, Michigan
*Horseless Carriage (Model S. Ford, Children and
    Animals—Sunday Afternoon)*, relief, limestone

United States Post Office, Sandwich, Illinois
The Family (Farm Animals), relief, terracotta

University of Michigan, Ann Arbor, Michigan
*Adventurer, Aesop, Hiawatha, Musicians,
    Naturalist, Scientists, Student Motif*, limestone;
    *Dream of the Young Girl, Dream of the Young
    Man*, bronze; and thirty untitled reliefs represent-
    ing God, Nature and Man, aluminum (Literature,
    Science and Arts Building)
American Eagle (Ann Arbor War Memorial Eagle)
    (Stadium)
Arthur H. Vandenberg, portrait relief (Rackham
    Memorial Building)
David Mathias Dennison, portrait relief
    (David M. Dennison Building)
Harrison M. Randall, portrait relief
    (Randall Laboratory)
William Andrew Paton, portrait relief
    (Paton Accounting Center)

University of Michigan-Dearborn, Dearborn, Michigan
*Siberian Ram** (Fair Lane Garden)

**University of Nebraska Medical Center, Omaha,
    Nebraska**
*Black Elk: Homage to the Great Spirit**
    (McGoogan Library of Medicine)

University of Virginia, Charlottesville, Virginia
Tracy W. McGregor, portrait relief
    (Tracy W. McGregor Library)

**Van Andel Museum Center of the Public Museum
    of Grand Rapids, Michigan**
Flying Wild Geese

Vero Beach Center for the Arts, Vero Beach, Florida
*Victory Eagle (American Eagle)**

**Vesterheim Norwegian American Museum,
    Decorah, Iowa**
Siesta (Reclining Lamb)

Victor Saroki and Associates, Birmingham, Michigan
*Fountain of Eternal Life**

Washington County Bank, Blair, Nebraska
*Black Elk: Homage to the Great Spirit**

Way Elementary School, Bloomfield Hills, Michigan
*The Boy and Bear**

Wayne State University, Detroit, Michigan
Tracy W. McGregor, portrait relief (Tracy W.
    McGregor Memorial Conference Center)
William John Stapleton, Jr., M.D., portrait relief
    (Shiffman Medical Library)

William Beaumont Hospital, Royal Oak, Michigan
The Family Protected by Healing Herbs, relief,
    aluminum
William Beaumont, M.D., portrait relief, copper-
    patinated bronze

30 North Building, 30 N. Saginaw, Pontiac, Michigan
Chief Pontiac, relief

*Note: The Marshall Fredericks Sculpture Museum at
Saginaw Valley State University also houses hundreds
of plaster models, medals, miniatures, jewelry,
armatures, tools, molds, drawings, photographs, and
archival materials. For more information, refer to
the essay by Barbara Heller "The Marshall M.
Fredericks Sculpture Museum" and the Selected
Bibliography.*

Contributors

A close friend and admirer of Marshall Fredericks, **William A. Bostick** met the artist shortly after World War II when Bostick was appointed administrator and secretary of the Detroit Institute of Arts—a position he held for thirty years, during which he worked closely with Edgar Richardson. Bostick holds a B.S. in graphic communication management from Carnegie Tech and an M.A. in art history from Wayne State University. He has been a typographer and advertising designer and designed many of the DIA publications during his tenure there. Watercolor painting and calligraphy are his passions in life.

The youngest daughter of Marshall Fredericks, **Suzanne P. Fredericks** first worked with her father on this book twenty-five years ago. She holds an M.A. in art history, with a certificate in art conservation, from New York University's Institute of Fine Arts. Currently active as a paintings conservator, Ms. Fredericks serves on the board of the Marshall M. Fredericks Sculpture Museum.

Marcy Heller Fisher, author of *The Outdoor Museum: The Magic of Michigan's Marshall M. Fredericks* (Detroit: WSU Press, 2001) and *Fired Magic: A Touring Tale of Detroit's Pewabic Pottery* (Detroit: WSU Press, 2003), holds an A.B. from the University of Michigan and an M.S. in education from Indiana University. She retired from a career in urban education to devote her efforts to writing, civil rights, and educational issues.

Michaele Duffy Kramer is a figurative sculptor living and working in Port Huron, Michigan. Her mother was Fredericks's student at Kingswood School Cranbrook in the 1930s, which led to Ms. Kramer's much-cherished relationship with the artist. Her work can be found at sites in St. Clair and Macomb counties. She recently finished an over life-size Indian family grouping for the city of Wyandotte and serves on the board of the Marshall M. Fredericks Sculpture Museum.

Barbara Heller is head conservator at the Detroit Institute of Arts. She joined the staff at the DIA in 1976, after having worked at the Palazzo Pitti in Florence, Italy. A graduate of the Museum Management Institute, at the University of California at Berkeley, she has academic credentials earned at Olivet College, the University of Michigan, Wayne State University, and Harvard University. A member of the board of the Marshall M. Fredericks Sculpture Museum since its inception in l988, she currently serves as secretary and collections committee chair.

Director of the Detroit Institute of Arts from 1945 to 1962, **Edgar P. Richardson** later served as director of the Winterthur Museum of American Art and as president of the board of the Pennsylvania Academy of the Fine Arts. A prominent art historian, he was editor of the *American Art Quarterly* from 1938 to 1967. Before his death in 1985, he published numerous articles and books, including *Painting in America: From 1502 to the Present* (New York: Thomas Y. Crowell Company, 1965) and *Charles Willson Peale and His World* (New York: Harry N. Abrams, 1982).

Samuel Sachs II was educated at Harvard and New York University's Institute of Fine Arts. He has been a museum professional his entire career, with posts in Minneapolis and Detroit, where he was director of the Detroit Institute of Arts from 1985 to 1997. A native New Yorker, he is presently director of the Frick Collection.

Robin R. Salmon is vice president and curator of sculpture at Brookgreen Gardens, where, since 1975, she has overseen its comprehensive collection of American representational sculpture. She came to know Marshall Fredericks as a sculptor through her job as a curator, and eventually became a friend of both Fredericks and his wife Rosalind. She worked closely with the artist during his twenty-four years as a trustee of Brookgreen Gardens.

MaryAnn Wilkinson is curator of modern and contemporary art at the Detroit Institute of Arts, where she has been a member of the curatorial staff since 1984. She first met Marshall Fredericks while serving as coordinator and research assistant for the major international exhibition, "Design in America: The Cranbrook Vision 1925–1950."

Photo/Illustration Credits

The publisher gratefully acknowledges all those who provided photographs for this book. Every attempt has been made to trace and contact copyright holders and gain permission for this use. Errors or omissions brought to the publisher's attention will be remedied in future editions. Photographs/illustrations not listed below were originally in the Marshall Fredericks Studio collection, now located in the Marshall M. Fredericks Sculpture Museum archives, where all images used in the book are available for viewing.

©Ingemar Aourell, Sweden: figs. 340–342

Hemstead de Aquero: fig. 138

Arnold Studios, Birmingham, Michigan: figs. 124, 140–144, 147, 151, 370–372

Elmer L. Astleford: figs. 125, 128, 135, 139, 178–180

Dirk Bakker: pl. 5; figs. 101, 105, 110, 157, 192, 217, 388, 389, 394, 397, 399, 403

Molly Barth, sculptor's assistant: pl. 28; figs. 319, 320, 328, 332, 333, 348, 350, 355, 356; line drawing for embossed gazelle on hardcover

Collection of Brookgreen Gardens, Pawleys Island, South Carolina: pl. 25

Win Brunner: fig. 137

Gary Bublitz-Bublitz Photography: jacket cover, pls. 1, 3, 6; figs. 102, 104, 109

Ralph Calder and Associates, Inc: figs. 358, 366

Campbell-Ewald Company: figs. 115, 369

Richard Clapp Photographic, Inc.: figs. 4, 18, 41, 47–49, 67–70, 75, 76, 79–81, 145, 146, 206, 218, 221–224, 226, 232, 269, 276, 291, 292, 301, 302 (bottom), 303, 304, 306–309, 311–314, 398

Joe Clark/TimePix: figs. 172, 236, 379, 380

Cleveland Institute of Art: figs. 1, 2

Courtesy of The Cleveland Museum of Art: figs. 9, 10, 13, 14, 16, 19–21, 24

©The Courier-Journal, Louisville, Kentucky: fig. 116

Courtesy of Cranbrook Archives, Cranbrook Educational Community, Bloomfield Hills, Michigan: figs. 17, 22, 23, 25–29, 31–40, 43–46, 50–62, 64–66, 72–74, 77, 78, 83, 85–98, 188–191, 193–196, 300, 405

Harvey Croze: figs. 119, 120, 126, 127, 129–132, 134, 150, 152–156

The Dallas Morning News: fig. 216

Bill Day: fig. 415

Detroit Free Press: fig. 160

Rosalind C. Fredericks: figs. 337, 339, 349, 351, 363, 364

Maurice C. Hartwick: pls. 11–13, 16–18; figs. 71, 181, 183–187, 197–203, 205, 207–210, 212–214, 219, 220, 222, 225, 227, 230, 231, 234, 235, 237–263, 265–268, 272–275, 277–281, 285–290, 293, 294, 297, 302 (top), 305, 377, 381, 391, 392, 396; photo used as basis for endpapers

©Chuck Heiney (for Frederik Meijer Gardens and Sculpture Park, Grand Rapids, Michigan): pl. 30; fig. 346

Franklin L. Hileman: fig. 63

Balthazar Korab Ltd: pls. 9, 14, 15, 19, 21, 23, 26, 27, 29, 31, 32; figs. 325–327, 347, 359

William Langley: fig. 215

Tad Merrick: pls. 4, 7, 8; figs. 103, 107, 108, 133, 211

The New Yorker Magazine ©1939: fig. 406

Ohio State University Photo Archives: figs. 164–166, 169

Phil Olsen: fig. 204

Rick Rhodes: pl. 2; figs. 99, 106, 111, 159

Saginaw Valley State University Information Service: figs. 357, 360–362, 365

Pat Seiter: figs. 335, 336, 344

Richard Shirk, Department of Photography, Ohio State University: figs. 8, 42, 149, 161–163, 170, 171, 173–177

G. Scott Slocum: figs. 329, 330, 331, 334, 338, 343, 345, 352–354, 373, 374

SmithGroup, Inc.: fig. 367

Tony Spina, Detroit Free Press/Tony Spina family: fig. 229

John R. Somers: figs. 100, 112, 113, 117, 158

Index

Page 265

Colophon

2,500 copies of *Marshall Fredericks, Sculptor* were printed on 100-pound Sterling Dull by University Lithoprinters, Inc.

The book was designed by William A. Bostick, who chose the computer typefaces: *Ex Ponto*, designed by Serbian calligrapher Jovica Veljovic, for the headings and display type, and *Trump Medieval*, designed by Georg Trump, for the text. Bostick thought that *Ex Ponto* complemented the curvaceous shapes of Marshall Fredericks's sculpture.